GW00728113

FLY FISHING IS EASY

FLY FISHING IS EASY

by

D. N. PUDDEPHA

('QUILL')

With 19 half-tone plates and 21 line illustrations

DAVID & CHARLES
NEWTON ABBOT

7153 4214 2

Printed in Great Britain by
Clarke, Doble & Brendon Ltd Plymouth
for David & Charles (Publishers) Ltd
South Devon House Railway Station
Newton Abbot Devon

CONTENTS

LIST OF PLATES

INTRODUCTION

FLY fishing *is* easy. It is far less complicated than most other methods of catching fish, float fishing and legering included. Coarse fishermen who try it are invariably surprised by its simplicity. Absolute beginners, too, soon realise with pleasure that it is by no means as difficult as they thought.

This book, then, is aimed at any coarse fishermen who feel they might like to take up fly fishing, and at beginners who want to start with fly rather than float. And I can assure them that anyone with a sound eye and arm can cast a fly and catch fish.

How do I know? Because I was once a raw beginner, and in the intervals between fly fishing I *am* a coarse fisherman.

It started like this. When I was a schoolboy I lived close to some small ponds tucked away in rural Worcestershire. There I learned how to fish for roach with float tackle and paste or worms for bait. My rod was a bean pole, my line was string. Only the float, cast and hook bore some resemblance to tackle proper. I taught myself to catch those roach—I had no close relations, no friends who fished.

Fishing was in my blood, though. My grandfather, who died years before my appearance, caught trout on the Staffordshire Blythe and the Devonshire Teign, and sea trout and salmon from the Dovey.

My mother conceded victory to angling at the end of my first summer holiday with the bean pole. My Christmas present that year was a fine 9ft green bamboo, coarse-fishing rod. My own family have since followed her good example, given angling best and bought me lots of tackle, bless their hearts. More important, they've sent me off to the water cheerfully and given me many an uproarious welcome home (especially when I've had a salmon or two!).

I threw a trout fly for the first time on the upper Dovey where trout were fairly plentiful and free rising. I remember distinctly the fly was an overdressed Snipe and Purple and the rod was my 9ft bamboo. Totally unsuitable? Yes, but remember, at that stage I was young, impecunious and absolutely fresh to fishing, let alone fly fishing. Nor would my mother have been right to provide me with expensive equipment. Several of grandfather's rods reposed in safe keeping; I was too young at twelve to be entrusted with them.

Somehow I cast that very unnatural Snipe and Purple across a few yards of the shallow, bottle-green Dovey water. The new bamboo bent a fraction towards the tip as I propelled the fly across that likely stretch, and two troutlets jumped over it but never touched the hook. In the event, on that first Dovey holiday I caught all my trout on the worm, wisely suiting the method to the tackle.

If this book were not restricted to fly fishing I could have told some tales of worming for trout, spinning minnows for sea trout, prawning for salmon. It's all part of the game—when and where regulations permit—but of all lures the fly is the least fussy and sometimes the deadliest. I love it, and so will you if you follow my advice and try it.

First, then, let us talk of tackle. Nothing complicated. We are going to deal with fish ranging from trout of an ounce or two up to salmon of 20lb, maybe more. Which are you going to catch most frequently? Well, there are far more $\frac{1}{4}$lb trout in this world than 20lb salmon. So for your first fly rod I recommend a 9ft split-cane or glass rod with a stiffish action. This will deal with any trout, sea trout or salmon. What it will not deal with is too heavy a line or fly—say a size 1 sunk salmon fly on a GAG line, which is a typical early spring salmon fly rig. We will go into detail on this subject later.

A stiffish action rod is recommended for two reasons: it simplifies casting and enables you to hook speedy-taking fish better than the old-fashioned 'soft' action sunk fly rod. But 'stiffish' certainly does not mean a rod like a gun barrel cleaner or my old 9ft bamboo. Your ideal fly rod is resilient and flexible; you should feel some movement in the wood or glass right down to your hand on its butt when casting.

It shouldn't quiver unduly. It should feel at its best with ten yards or so of line out—and if you can afford it, get one with a spare top because ten-to-one you'll tread on it, or allow a cow to tread on it at some stage.

Happily, most tackle dealers are honest and helpful men; like the anglers they serve. Entrust your fly fishing future to one of them if you lack a friend to advise. The budget for your first outfit could be like this:

9ft split-cane or glass rod	£7 upwards (glass is cheaper)
3in metal fly reel	£2 upwards
30 yards HCH line spliced to 50 yards of backing	£3 upwards
Six 25 yard spools of nylon, 2-10lb breaking strain approx.	£1
Three dozen assorted dry and wet flies sizes 10-17 (Redditch scale)	£2
Scissors ('borrow' from sewing box)	nil
	approximate total £15

Not too alarming is it? It is assumed that you have some old trousers you won't mind ripping on the innumerable barbed wire fences which anglers inevitably encounter. Waterproofs and gum boots, too, are common to most men. When you decide you are going to like fly fishing, and in all weathers, you can always extend your wardrobe to sou'westers, light oilskins and thigh waders.

If you are a coarse fisherman you will already possess a net, disgorger, line grease and a spring balance. My trout balance goes up to 4lb and I've only once bumped it to its limit with a trout. These are the sort of extras whose importance ranks differently among fly fishermen. Personally, I rarely use a net when trouting, but I wouldn't be without a large, long-handled net when after sea trout, nor a small gaff with a priest end (to knock them on the head) for salmon. A triangular folding net is adequate for river trout: a larger, circular ring type better for reservoir trout or sea trout. So, to the basic needs costing you £15, the following extras can be added at little or no cost per item:

Landing net	10s to several guineas
Tobacco tin (to hold flies)	nil
Tin of grease (to float dry flies)	2s 6d

Piece of amadou (absorbent material to dry and clean soaked or fish-bloody flies) 2s
Bag . . . . 10s to several guineas

Later, when we are studying methods of searching many different types of water for the various fish which take fly, there will be further recommendations on rods and other gear. Enough, at this point, to assure you that you now possess all that's necessary in principle.

But before we begin talking flies and fish, let us first put the tackle together and make a cast or two on the back lawn or even across some open length of river.

Your rod may be a two or three-piece affair. I prefer a two-piece, but I cannot honestly say I've noticed much difference in the action as against a three-piece, though the latter will probably weigh slightly more and any extra ferrule is a possible source of future weakness. Let us assume you have acquired a sturdy two-piece with perfectly normal fittings. Slide the ferrules together gently, checking that the rings on both joints are in line. Always handle the rod by its ferrules—never twist or pull a sticking ferrule by handling the wood or glass itself. Remember, you are dealing with an expensive and relatively delicate article which deserves respect and will last a lifetime if you treat it sensibly.

Attach the reel to the fittings on the butt, in line with the rod rings, and pull the line off, threading it through *every* ring. Opinions on how best to join line to cast (as the nylon length between line and fly is known) are apt to differ from angler to angler. Most of us use a knot like this . . .

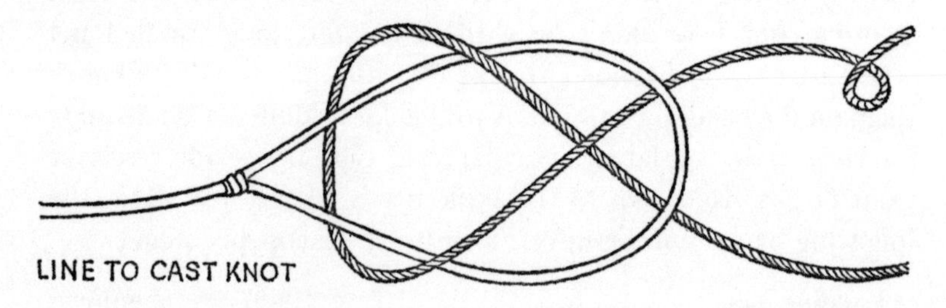

LINE TO CAST KNOT

. . . which helps to jam it in the loop of the cast.

The cast loop is easily achieved:

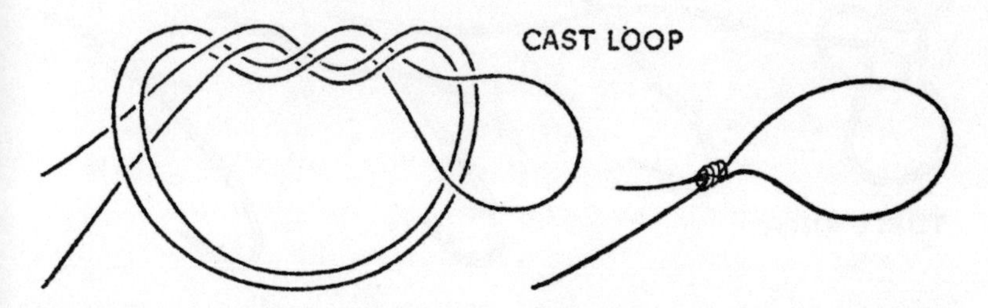

While we are fixing up tackle we might as well tie on a tapered cast. The alternative is a level cast, which is of the same breaking strain from line to fly. They can often be used, are obviously less trouble to prepare, and have the advantage of being without knots, which sometimes scare fish. But tapered casts are the rule, for the simple reason that they make casting and presentation of the fly much easier and more effective, especially when the wind is adverse. And when you hook a bush on the opposite bank you lose only your fly and a foot or so of a tapered cast.

A typical river cast would taper from 7lb b.s. nylon down to $2\frac{1}{2}$lb in several stages. Each section is knotted together like this:

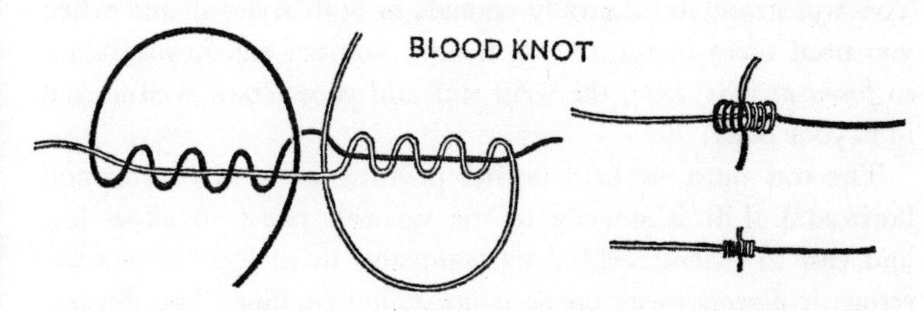

This is the blood knot and quite the neatest thing about my tackle. But don't forget that before using *any* cast you must give it a strong test pull. Always do this even after catching a small fish.

Your cast is tied, tapered to a slender $2\frac{1}{2}$lb breaking-strain point. We are now going to try a few practice casts without a fly attached but first I'll show you how to attach it and you can then break it off and see for yourself just how tough $2\frac{1}{2}$lb nylon is. Again, knots for this particular attachment are legion. Mine is illustrated overleaf.

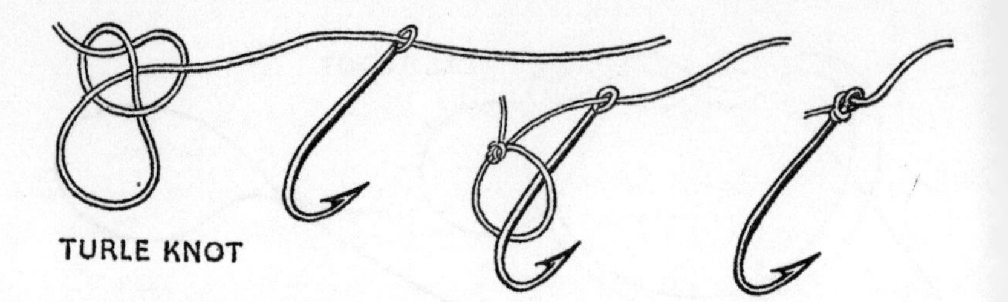
TURLE KNOT

It's called a Turle knot. Pull it tight and test it. Fish won't break it in open water if fingers can't. Now we can take it off and begin casting.

Pull two or three more yards of line from the reel. You will always handle the line close to the reel, and certainly between your reel and the butt ring which is the lowest on your rod. Now you have a length of line roughly equal to the length of the rod, and about two and a half yards of cast beyond it. Engrave this on your memory : your forearm is going to do the work. Tournament casters may use their arm and shoulder, leaning back and throwing half their body into a stupendous cast. Some old and wise brook fishermen are quite happy with a wrist-only action. You will graduate naturally enough to both styles if and when you need them in future. Right now, you are still in my hands so *forearm* it is; keep the wrist stiff and your elbow well tucked in to your body.

The rod must be held firmly, pointing in front of you and horizontal. Lift it smartly to the vertical, pause to allow line and cast to extend behind its point and then, equally smartly, return it *almost* to its previous horizontal position. The illustration opposite shows what I mean.

Make each cast a deliberate movement with a definite aiming point in front. Timing is all-important. A mite too quick and you tangle cast and fly on the forward movement; too slow, and you lose control and hit the thistles or the ground behind you.

To reach your destination on the golf course you may need several clubs. To reach a rising fish on the river you have only one rod but a number of different casting actions at your disposal. There will be more about these later, when the basic move-

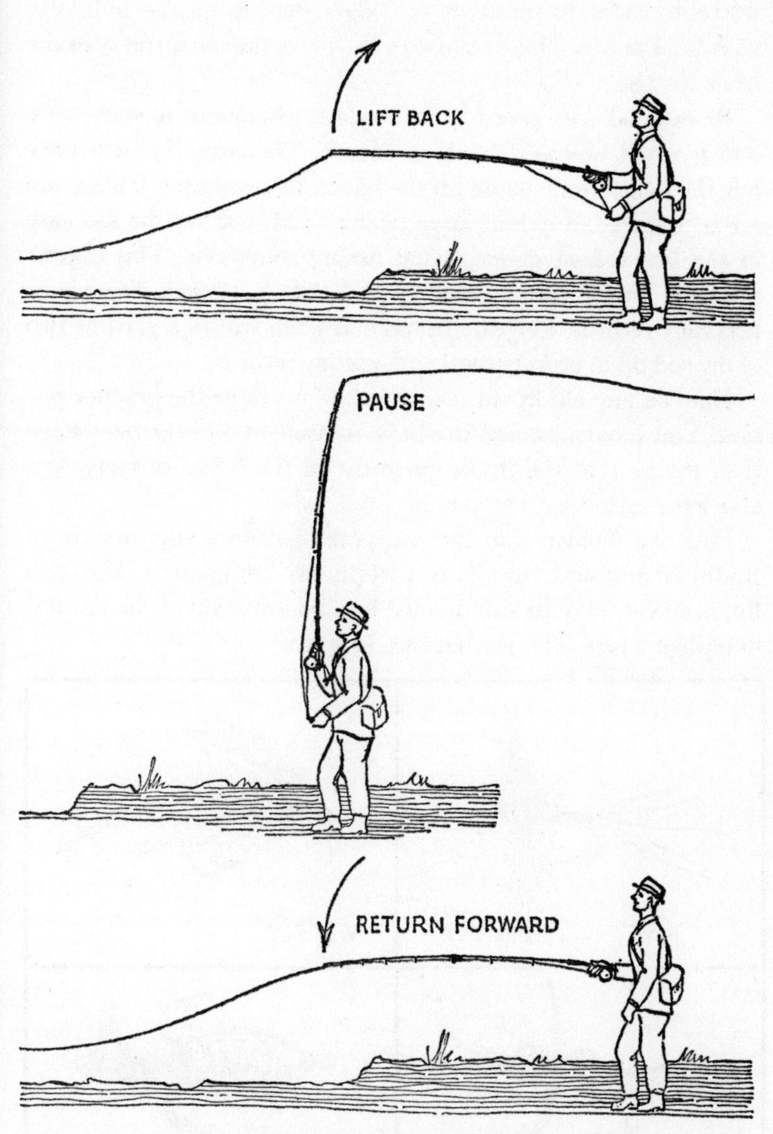

Casting: The three basic movements

ment has been practised sufficiently. I've always found it considerably easier to put a fly on target than to hit the bull's-eye with float tackle. The weight of a fly line acting on a rod does the work for you.

Be satisfied with seven or eight yards of line out to start with, and it won't be too difficult to handle. The more line you have out the longer your pause on the back cast should be. Unless you are a 'natural', anything over twelve yards will not be too easy in the first season under actual fishing conditions. This doesn't matter a bit for you are out to catch fish, not break distance or accuracy records. I've caught too many fish within a yard or two of my rod tip to be impressed with casting records.

Now tie any old fly on your cast and continue the practice session. You have mastered the basic movement and the next stage is to ensure that the fly drops softly on the water surface. Aim above the surface and keep at it.

Flies are divided into two categories: surface (the dry fly of tradition) and sunk (wet fly or nymph, also traditional). The sunk fly, however, may be sub-divided into an imitation of the natural nymph or a lure. This is what they look like:

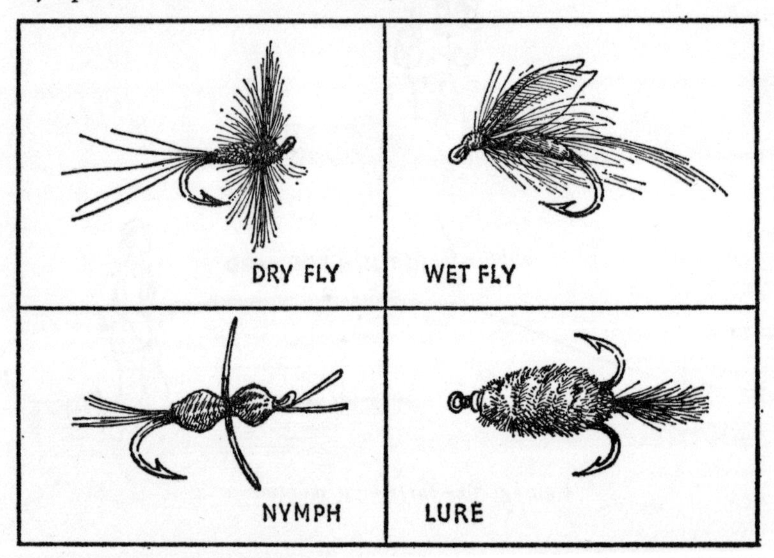

Most trout flies follow nature to a certain extent, most salmon flies are lures and none the worse for that. Entomology is undoubtedly fascinating (like championship casting) but expert knowledge of the subject won't catch you any fish your fellow anglers can't catch. The fly on or in the water catches the most fish, whatever artificial pattern it happens to be. That's an old, wise adage and, believe me, it applies particularly to salmon and sea trout fishing. These are creatures whose mood rather than appetite dictates the bag, whereas trout do go in for definite feeding periods on natural fly.

We shall be talking a lot about surface fly, sunk fly and lures in this book, and I want to leave you in no doubt about the differences between them, which are considerable.

When I talk of surface fly, I shall mean the imitation, maybe representation would be an apter description, of the duns (i e flies) which have hatched and are floating on the surface of river or lake. Below left, is a dun:

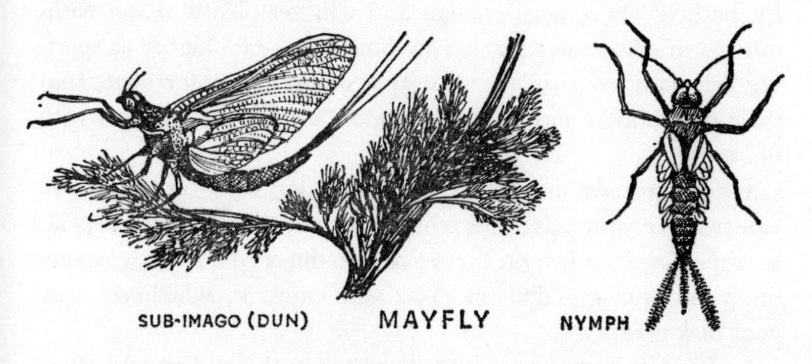

I shall also mean flies and other creatures which are not hatched from the water itself but fall upon it: the cowdung fly, the bluebottle, wingy ants, beetles and so on.

Sunk fly means the nymph of river and lake flies. It represents the underwater stage of the fly. Trout, grayling and some coarse fish feed a good deal more on nymphs and other underwater morsels than they do on the surface. Above right, is a nymph.

Lures may be intended to represent nymphs or small fish, normally the latter. And they can also be had in the form of shrimps, caterpillars and beetles. There are times and places for all three varieties of fly, and no order of merit save on some very sacred chalk or limestone waters where the rule is 'Dry Fly Only'.

River bred flies—whose eggs become nymphs, whose nymphs become duns, whose duns become spinners which have mated and laid their eggs in cycle—number hundreds of species over Britain as a whole. Books have been written about them. Fly patterns have been invented for most of them. Some anglers even seem to care more for the fly than the fish and become entomologist-anglers. You may eventually go the same way, but first learn how to master your tackle and take fish from any water. Specialisation, I am convinced, narrows the angling mind, fascinating though it may be. For this reason, although writing here of fly fishing only, I urge you to spin, to worm, to go coarse and sea fishing too and so gain the fullest enjoyment from the finest of sports.

Most anglers, I'm sure, have a secret wish to catch a trout on the fly, and a trout should be your first quarry. Sea trout can be difficult, and salmon much more expensive—although you'll go for both if you're keen enough and will get plenty of fun without too much extravagance. Grayling I now rate higher as sporting fish than trout (in the same rivers) and it is unfortunate that their distribution and fly-taking season is limited compared with the trout.

Once you have mastered the art of taking trout on the fly you can transfer your affections where you will. Fly fishing, I repeat, is easy. *Catching* fish on the fly is sometimes equally easy, sometimes entrancingly difficult. You will enjoy it, whichever way your luck goes.

So let us now make a start with trout; in theory first and afterwards in practice. And let us be grateful that there isn't a county in Britain completely devoid of trout.

CHAPTER ONE

TROUT: *Small River—Sunk Fly Downstream*

THEORY

THE best nursery for a trout fly fisherman is a small river; that is, a river whose width can be covered, bank to bank, by one exceptional cast, say a maximum of twenty yards. It should have some interesting lengths without bushes or trees along its banks, although trout and a certain amount of cover always go together. A brook can be difficult owing to its very smallness and on a big river, like a reservoir or lake, distance casting *may* come in handy at times; trout aren't always within a beginner's reach.

A small river offers space for casting, a depth varying from inches to four or five feet and a fair population of trout whose weight will range—on average—from an ounce or two up to a pound. Commonly these rivers produce bags of four, three and, best of all, two-to-the-pound trout.

Some will have moorland origins, like the Devonshire Exe. But the Exe flows in its middle reaches through a pastoral valley and this means slightly better feeding for its trout. There are plenty of ¾lb fish and at times they rise freely.

It pays to let the river and the wind, if any, do as much work as possible for you when fishing the fly. Surface fly fishing upstream—known as dry fly fishing—is much harder work than fishing a sunk fly across and down the stream. So let the first outing of spring, mid-March or a week or two later, be an exploratory one with sunk fly.

Trout seasons vary from place to place in Britain. Many rivers open on 1 March, particularly in Scotland and Wales. There are, however, waters which do not feel a line until late April, though they can be fished into October. Remember, whatever the opening date, this time of year is usually decidedly cool. The trout are likely to be lean after their winter spawning. They have mostly been feeding underwater for the past four or five months. They will not be lying in the fast, shallow water; nor will they be deep down the pools and slacks like so many coarse fish. Search for them in moderately flowing water, and the fly should do most of that searching for you.

Not many trout will deign to rise on a cold, cutting day in late March with the river at spring level, but who can resist making a start? For this type of river and fishing the tackle to which I've introduced you is ideal. The old style of wet fly fishing called for a sunk line, but you needn't worry about that. You have a floating line on your reel and that is easier to lift off the water when making a fresh cast. Your tapered nylon cast may be inclined to float, too, especially the heavier top length. I suggest you make up a cast three yards long from a yard each of 6lb, 4½lb and 3lb nylon. When it's attached to your line give it a good stretch to straighten it and an equally vigorous rub in the mud or fine gravel at the river's edge, and repeat the dose whenever it shows signs of re-floating. You won't do too badly if two-thirds of the cast goes under.

When trout are feeding on nymphs they may take them almost anywhere between the river bed and its surface, but it's a certain bet *most* of their feeding will be done nearer the surface. Consequently you need not try to hook the bed of the river, even if the current allowed your fly to sink sufficiently.

You must send your sunk fly across and downstream, allowing the main current to carry it to the limit of the cast and swing it gently across towards your bank. You may be on the bank, or wading, it makes no difference; but *always* select the stance which gives you the best chance of covering trout (placing the fly over them) without arousing their suspicion.

The advantage of this form of fly fishing is that even a moderate river flow will straighten out the worst of casts and fish the fly for a short distance in a manner not unlike the action of some nymphs. If a trout grabs the fly when it is working properly, it may hook itself or at least give a pull which can be felt and struck in return.

Fly sizes needn't vary much over the whole season. As a general rule you will use them a size or two bigger in spring and autumn than in the low water conditions of high summer. What size? Let's say Nos 12 to 14 (Redditch scale) for the first attempt if the water is high and slightly coloured. These sizes may still be a couple of digits too small—only experience will ease the pangs of selection. Every season, by the way, many a good trout grabs a large salmon fly and the same greedy fish are caught on size 17 hooks—you can drop half a dozen of those on a sixpence.

Surface flies are tied to float with the aid of cock's hackles. Sunk flies are tied with hen hackles which are softer and more absorbent. Gimmicks to ensure deep sinking include tying flies with lead or lead wire on their bodies, using small double hooks and soaking them in a glycerine mixture. I pinch them in a dab of mud and then waggle them back and forth in the water—or just spit on them!

Always study the water before fishing. Weigh up in your mind where you want the fly to descend and what you will do when a trout is hooked. Move slowly into position to make the first cast, which can be as short as you like. If you try immediately to reach the far bank of the river all the trout lying across the line of your cast will be scared, and in turn scare others below.

Remember, if you want to cast a fly eight yards in front of you it must first travel a similar distance to the rear. When you have only eight yards clear space for your back cast and want to extend forward distance this can be done by shooting line. It's very simple. Pull an extra yard or two of line from the reel, holding it firmly above the loops of slack line and, as the rod tip begins to feel the full weight of your extended line when moving forward and downward, let go the extra line. It will rustle up through the rod rings and the extra yard or two distance is achieved. Shooting line in this way is the first of those little extras which will contribute to your eventual expertise. And it delivers the fly much more gently.

Search the river cast by cast, gradually lengthening line until your fly drops as near as you can manage in the main stream. It is easier to cast across river from the shallow side. This will ensure proper fishing of the fly. When you hook a trout it can be played into quiet water and drawn to the net.

What fly is best for this fishing at this time of year? The correct answer is the fly which looks most likely to suit conditions, the fly in which you have most confidence. But as this is not particularly helpful to someone totally new to fly fishing, I will suggest some patterns, and you—like every other trout angler—will gradually compile your own favourite list.

Before suggesting your choice, let me emphasise I am in earnest over this business of the fly. *Presentation* is vastly more important than *imitation*. There will always be times when trout ignore one fly and accept another and you should be prepared to change patterns to try and meet their taste; but never, never become a slave to the fly-box. The angler who spends his day changing flies is constantly losing good fishing time. If it entertains him, that is reasonable enough. If the trout exasperate him and he complains of the lack of weight in his bag at the end of the day, I have less sympathy.

First fly on my cast in the spring is a Greenwell's Glory, virtually standard fare for March and April trout, sunk or surface. Hardly a river runs without some large, dark Olives at this season and the Greenwell is a close enough representation of this excellent natural. The March Brown is my second choice, even on rivers whose hatch of this fly is apparently non-existent. Fly patterns and types of tying vary according to localities, of course. In Wales, the Welsh border and the West Country, I should expect to find flies tied with substantial bodies and fairly full hackles. In the north and Scotland, the general trend is for a thinner article altogether, particularly on well-thrashed rivers like the Clyde.

Do not hurry to reach the river in spring. Ten to half-past is full early and precious little will be missed if the tackle is taken down at tea-time—say five o'clock. To be fishing at the most likely time, eat lunch before midday or after 2 pm and concentrate during the period of relatively highest air temperature.

I prefer what the Irish call a 'soft' day at any time of year. Some cloud and a warm west wind are the conditions river trout like best. A hard day when the sun glares and a high wind chases wavelets downstream is not encouraging. I prefer to fish between showers rather than endure constant rain, not only for my own comfort but because I'm convinced the trout, too, prefer showers to downpours. Naturally a rising barometer and temperature are preferable, if you can choose your day, but whatever the conditions you have the satisfaction of knowing that trout are there and they may take the fly at any time. Be consoled, on one of the tougher days, by a brace caught with difficulty. Maybe they were better deserved than the six brace an easy day provided.

PRACTICE

There's the river. It's decidedly cool, but we could have picked a worse day. We'll leave the car in the farmyard and stroll across the meadow to set up your tackle on the river banks. The Exe looks surprisingly clear and fast flowing at this time of year, and bare along its banks here, which is why I have selected it for your first outing. April comes in next week, but who would believe it looking at the countryside?

There's a brisk wind blowing and I suspect those black clouds up the valley are going to hurl down some sleet on our handsome deerstalkers. Never mind, the north-westerly wind will suit your casting nicely here since the river flows due south.

You are probably wondering what fly to attach to your cast. Olives always appear on this river so let's have a No 12 Greenwell up. If your casting goes well, we'll double your chances later on by tying a second fly on the cast—a dropper we call it.

Time to start. It's almost eleven o'clock and the sun has warmed us up a little. If we stroll downstream a couple of hundred yards we shall find a good length of trout water. It's narrow and very fast-flowing at the top, gradually widening out and calming down. The main current is always within easy reach for an angler in thigh waders. From top to bottom of this stretch is about 150 yards, but we'll give the first fifty yards a miss—although you could usefully concentrate there later in the year under warm, low water conditions.

We won't need those nice new thigh waders on this occasion, we've come here to try and hook trout on the fly, not to tread on them. Never wade until absolutely necessary in order to cover the water properly. And never continue wading for the sake of it unless, like a cow in August, you insist on keeping cool that way.

I see you've straightened your cast, soaked it and tested the fly attachment knot. Now drop the fly in the water at your feet and draw it gently upstream. This will soon show you whether it's tied on correctly, horizontally in line with the cast so that it moves through the water on a level plane. It is important, I assure you. This is what I mean:

Fly on correct plane *Wrong! Badly knotted*

Your first cast or two seems a bit strange, but by lunchtime you'll feel like a veteran. The first practical advice I offer is this: we are on the right bank of the river (facing downstream) and you are looking across to the opposite bank and trying to cast your fly rather too squarely. The current is nipping along even here, away from the head of the pool, and whisking your fly round much too fast and close to the surface. Do a half-right turn, army style, and cast across and down.

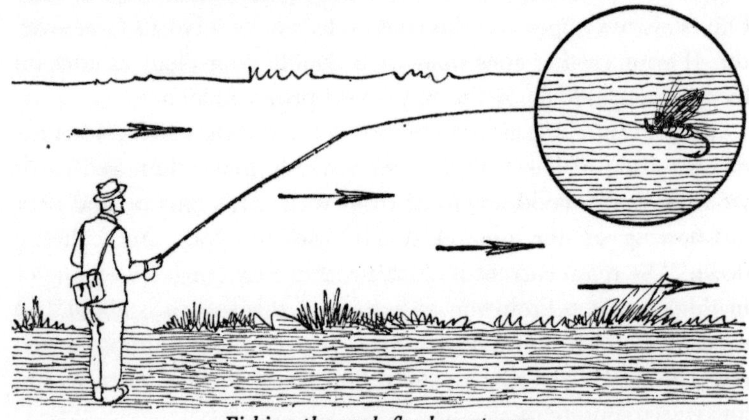

Fishing the sunk fly downstream

This ensures that the fly swings steadily, almost lazily, in an arc downstream of you. Keep your rod point motionless while the fly is fishing round, pause a moment when it ceases to swing and then lift the rod *gently* a foot or two upwards. This imparts a perfectly natural, attractive movement to the fly which sometimes brings an offer; and it lifts a yard or two of line clear of the water ready for the next cast.

Try and achieve a steady rhythm in your casting, but do not become a slave to the act of casting a given length of line. The river is constantly changing as you fish your way along it and the cast and manner you choose to fish must vary too.

You have now made eleven casts, all with the same length of line, and you haven't moved downstream a yard! Sunk fly fishing in spring is essentially an exploratory business. The flies must be taken to the trout, the fish won't come to you. If you were salmon fishing you would take a full step between each cast. Generally, I shuffle downstream a foot at a time between trout casts. Keep moving. The most successful angler on these moorland-type rivers is the man who casts most often and moves quickly, though quietly as a bankside shrew.

When I mentioned rhythm, I meant a clean pick-up of line at the end of each cast followed by the forward throw. Sunk flies fish more effectively when soaked and it's surprising how a few false casts will dry out a fly. A false cast is simply a means of getting out more line and for changing direction. You send the fly forward but keep it in the air and repeat the casting movement. Some anglers I've watched are false casters ad infinitum. Don't copy them.

You're moving quietly, casting is going well, all we want now is a trout.

Did you feel something? I had a suspicion your line tightened momentarily as you began to lift. Trout will often take a fly incredibly gently and let it go before our slow human reflexes start operating. Step back a foot upstream and repeat the cast. If the trout hasn't seen you it may have several tries for that juicy Greenwell.

Well done! You struck him automatically as you began lifting for the next cast, but it isn't a trout you've got there. Reel in quickly, lead him gently into the shallows and I'll explain.

This little chap, about four inches long, is a salmon parr. See the delicate little barred stripes down his sides? Those are known as parr markings and they spell the word 'illegal' to anglers everywhere. This is a salmon in the making—just over a year old and most likely to be in the river another year before going off to sea. Parr are greedy little fellows and a handful of unscrupulous fishermen could do some damage to a river's stock if they killed all they caught. Hence they are protected by law.

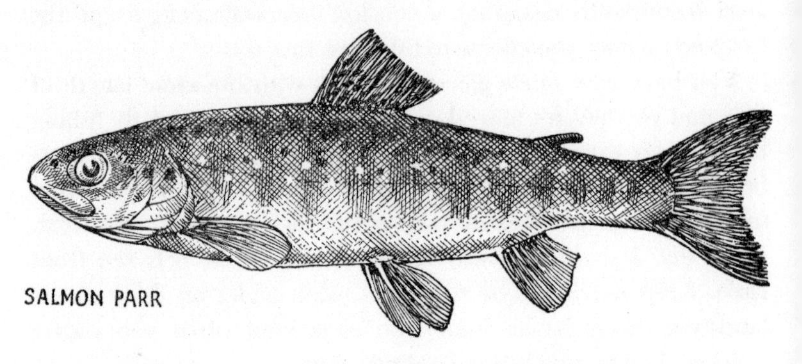

SALMON PARR

Now for your first lesson in unhooking a fish—and this one is well hooked in the top of its jaw. Wet your hand and lay the parr across it, curving your palm slightly and holding your thumb over the fish in case it struggles. Exert no pressure on its sides. Get a firm grip on the fly and ease its point back the way it went through, taking good care not to jerk the parr's head unduly. Very rarely is it necessary to use any force when unhooking a fly-caught fish. Many parr and small trout do not need handling at all. Draw them to hand, run your fingers down the cast, grip the fly and let their first struggle free it for you.

If by unfortunate chance you hook a fish deeply and cause bleeding from its gills, be merciful and kill it promptly. Nature is not kind to wounded creatures and the thought of a small trout or parr gradually drifting downstream, unable to fend for itself, is one that should be uppermost in a sportsman's mind. When you have caught a sizeable fish you wish to keep, kill it immediately. It has given you sport and must be treated with respect. Grip the fish firmly and hit its head *hard* on the landing net handle or a convenient stone; or use a sturdy piece of metal or wood known as a 'priest', with which to administer the last rites. An alternative method, suitable only for a smallish trout, is to insert your thumb into its mouth and bend its head smartly upwards, breaking the backbone.

Here's that sleetstorm I promised you. Let's get under those willows and have a bite of lunch until it passes. Prop the rod up carefully, out of range of clumsy feet. Make sure the fly is anchored on that tiny ring the makers kindly provided just above the handle.

On second thoughts, give me your tackle and I can be tying on a second fly—the dropper—a No 10 March Brown. It can go a yard from the tail fly, as we call the one on the end of the cast, and the drill is to cut the cast at its final knot, re-tying it with the same blood knot and leaving one free end several inches long. Make it the stronger section of cast for safety. Here's how:

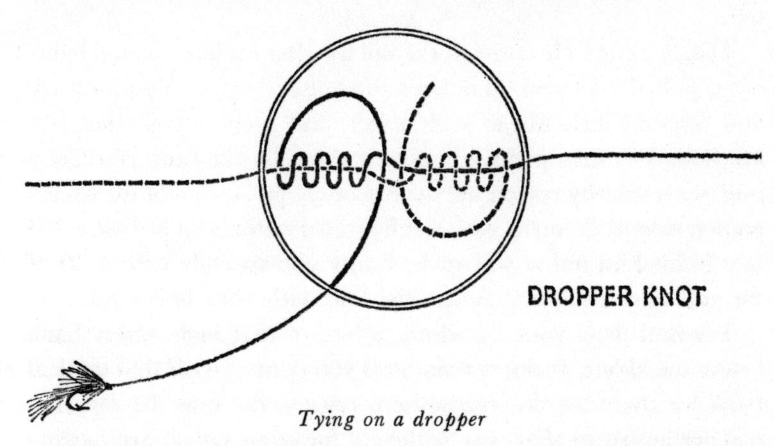

Tying on a dropper

Note that I'm rubbing some pleasant-smelling, muddy paste on the upper part of your cast and down to the dropper. This will ensure it sinks when you start again. Handling nylon often tends to 'grease' it a little. The mixture is simply a blend of Fuller's Earth and glycerine, but it will sink anything.

Now we'll walk on down and try a favourite run of mine at every stage of the season. The main current rushes down the middle of the river, spreading out until it flows under a couple of alder bushes which lean out drunkenly from the far bank. Below the alders the run deepens to five or six feet under a high bank.

Trout are greedy fish always on the look-out for food. But they prefer not to exert themselves, and choose places to hover in the current with the least expenditure of energy. Absolutely slack water is seldom worth fishing in a river, except at night when the trout may be cruising round after sedges and moths. At this time of year the easy flow is most attractive to them.

It's a quarter to one and should be just about the best time of the day. Did you see that tiny splash a couple of yards above the first alder and two yards nearer midstream? So there's at least one feeding trout at home.

Should be coming over him now, I think. Oh, but what a cast! You slammed it down on the surface like a sailor hurling a rope. Still, you can hardly be expected to keep calm making your first cast over a feeding fish, though you'll soon learn to steel yourself.

There, a tug! He came to the tail fly after all like greased lightning, pulled your rod tip down and vanished again. You must try and respond instantly to such a fish, and even at your best you are bound to miss plenty. Everyone does. By the time you feel a pull, see a splashy rise on the surface or catch a gleam of the trout's golden side as he turns with the fly underwater, you are often too late to hit him unless you strike firmly and speedily with a lift of the rod and a slight draw on the line with your left hand.

Try and drop your fly within a foot of that high, sandy bank below the alders. It doesn't matter if you bounce it off that vertical bank for there are no obstructions; later in the year the cast that reaches across in that way is deadly for trout which are looking for morsels on the surface.

You're into a trout! Hooked by that fierce strike, he's dancing wildly on the surface. A leap, another and another! Ah, that's better, he's gone downstream and deep. Let the rod tip absorb every throbbing pull. Hold it well up. *No* slack line, whatever you do. Reel in a few yards. Your trout is on his side, head just showing on the surface. Master him steadily and here's the net. Got him!

A nice fish but rather thin. Too much head for his body—but you don't care. There's nothing like your first trout, except your first salmon. Knock him on the head quickly; I'm sure you want him for your supper though, candidly, I'd rather have a kipper at this stage of the season. He weighs 10oz. Three months later you might have met him as a three-quarter-pounder.

What a picture a trout of any size makes. Those golden sides, the red and yellow spots; the fight they give and the way they jump. It's all memorable. By the way, while you are studying your trout, etching it in memory, let me explain why it kicked up such a fuss when you hooked it. When you felt it and struck, you held your line firmly, pulled the rod tip right back over your head and refused to budge an inch. Trout always fight wildly when held hard and may sometimes be bullied straight over the net. But many lightly-hooked fish are lost by this same firmness. Treat them 'suently', as old hands in Devon say: sweetly, gently and persuasively.

Right, you've been admiring your prize long enough. Now, back to the river to catch another. A brace is twice as good as one trout, and I have a harmless fetish about 'making the brace' whenever possible. It's a form of competition with the fish, whereas I seldom feel any inclination to try and better the catches of my fellow anglers.

Well done, there's number two on. A smaller fish, but nicely handled. Here's the net, you slip it under him.

Good work. I thought for a moment you were going to chase the fish round the river with the net as if you were butterfly hunting. It's quite common to miss your shot if the trout isn't totally played out. Ideally, it should be on its side and really beaten before being pulled over the well sunk net. One smooth lift and it's yours. Naturally it depends on the calibre of the trout. You will take liberties with quarter-pounders but treat their elder brethren thrice that weight with respect.

Time flies on the river and it's now half-past three and still too breezy for comfort. We have had the best of the day, although if you are still keen there's always a chance of a hungry or plain daft fish! I rate dusk the best time of day at most times of year for all the fish which take fly: but a spring dusk on the river ought to be calm and warm, which this afternoon certainly is not. All the same, you've had a very fair day. Even the experts find things tough going in March, particularly where trout aren't too plentiful. Trout have to share this stretch of river with innumerable dace and some choice grayling.

Here's a polythene bag to wrap the trout in and keep their slime from covering your tackle bag. And when the admiration society at home has ceased to marvel at your brace I'll show you how to prepare them for a meal. It's quite simple. I work over a sheet of newspaper, grasping the trout by its back and inserting a sharp, pointed knife in its vent near the tail. I run the knife right up to the gills and proceed to pull the guts out intact. Then I scrape what looks like black blood and is actually the trout's kidneys away from the backbone. I do *not* wash my fish under the tap at any stage after death. Removal of any soil, blood or grass, is easy enough with a damp rag or a piece of paper.

Some cooks cut off the trout's head. So do I if they are too large for the grill, frying pan or baking dish. Otherwise I leave them intact for the sake of appearance and to stop them curling open if cooked under fierce heat.

Your fish, by the way, will be white-fleshed and not very exciting. I rarely eat a river trout these days when I can catch the better fed, pink-fleshed specimens from reservoirs. You, too, will develop your prejudices!

CHAPTER TWO

TROUT: *Small River—Surface Fly Upstream*

THEORY

THIS is dry fly fishing—the half-knowledgeable refer to it with awe: 'Dry fly fishing, I suppose?' The very expression confers a touch of snobbery to the practice, an air of doing the right thing. This is a pity because at least one form of fishing the fly presents greater technical difficulties—the upstream nymph—and although dry fly is to me the most fascinating art of all I do not consider it is sportingly on a higher plane than any other means of taking fish.

On the willingness of trout and other fish to take tiny morsels off the surface, morsels which even numbered by the score can scarcely constitute a square meal, hinges the whole business of fly fishing. We know we can catch as many, and larger fish on worm or minnow but there is something magical about dropping a tiny, daintily dressed hook tied to represent the natural object, and actually persuading a fish to take it.

Surface fly offers the very real advantage of something to look at. You might compare it to fishing with a float, and sunk fly to legering with the line over your fingers, waiting to feel a fish pull. The rise, when a trout sips the fly down, may be a mere dimple or a lively splash but there is no doubt about it, and the strike which follows, if correctly timed, ought to be generally more successful than responding to plucks at a sunk lure.

A fly doesn't *have* to be cast upstream or downstream, surface or sunk. There are no hard and fast rules. In practice, you will fish a sunk fly downstream in the early part of the year because it slows up presentation of the fly in high water, shows it moving gently and, what's more, shows it before the fish see anything of the cast or line. You will fish surface fly mainly up and across the river, approaching trout from behind in order not to alarm them and allowing the fly to drift over their noses like the natural. You can throw a sunk fly upstream—very deadly this—and less often you can throw a surface fly downstream; say you want to drift it under some low, overhanging tree branches. Normally this is a one-chance-only cast, resulting in a scare for the fish when the fly is retrieved upstream.

Upstream surface fly fishing on rivers of moderate to fast current is a quicker business altogether than downstream fishing. The fly must not *drag*, by which I mean it must not be pulled off its direct downstream course by faster or slower currents operating on the cast or line, and you should always be gathering line with your free hand in order to be instantly in touch when you rise a fish. The latter practice you should develop instinctively. Certainly you will want to put matters right when you have struck empty air a few times instead of the fish because there was too much slack line ungathered.

Drag is a tougher adversary altogether, but it can be overcome, with patience and practice. Surprisingly few fish will take a dragging fly—sedge fishing is an exception we'll deal with later on. Your object is always to fish the fly in the most natural manner possible, which means it must come tripping down the runs without hindrance from the cast, circle slowly round a back eddy where trout cruise in the scum picking out fly leisurely, or perhaps drift three or four yards along some canal-like stretch of water over several fish.

To achieve this you must always aim to cast a slack line—sometimes a very slack line if you want to drop your fly well beyond the main current on the nose of a feeding trout. The illustration opposite shows what I mean.

The wriggle in line and cast will 'take up' and prevent any dragging pull on the fly.

How do you put a wriggle into your line? It's not as difficult as it sounds. Very often if there's any breeze at all from any direction except directly behind your casting arm it will do the job for you, creating a bend in the nylon cast. If you want to ensure a foot or so of slack, give the rod tip a sideways shake just after delivering the forward casting movement and while the fly is descending towards the water. Sometimes you may find it easier to aim the fly at a point slightly beyond its intended target and then pull it back while it is still in the air.

Whatever you do, remember the natural fly does not hit the surface of the river with a flop—indeed the river-bred dun emerges through the surface film and sits on top while its wings dry out preparing to fly. There is every reason to go on practising

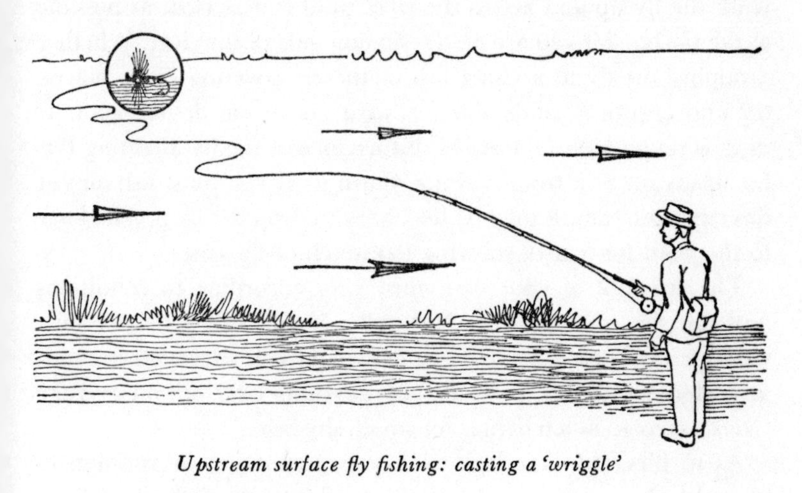

Upstream surface fly fishing: casting a 'wriggle'

casting until you can drop your floating fly on the water like a piece of thistledown.

Surface fly is effective at all times of year, even the months when trout are out of season it will take grayling and certain coarse fish. I chose a sunk fly in the chilly conditions described in the preceding section, but the moment the weather warms up I turn eagerly to surface fly. It's worth remembering that in the average British river or lake, trout may be persuaded to pop up and take a fly even when no rises are to be seen. Casting a surface fly over all the likely places in a river often brings surprisingly good results.

Your approach to the river, as always, must be cautious. Whereas you began casting your sunk fly immediately, it will now pay you to study the course of the current, the likeliest places for trout to lie and the *exact* position of any rises there may be. Sunk fly fishing, as you've realised by now, is slightly indiscriminate by comparison. You can afford to shrug off the occasional clumsy cast. Not so with the surface fly. Aim for the bull every time, not just for the inner rings.

Your tackle was chosen as a dual-purpose rig. The 9ft rod and other paraphernalia are perfectly suitable for upstream fishing: *you* will have to do the necessary adapting.

Fish the nearer water first and, as line is lengthened, gradually work the fly up and across the river until it is as close as possible to the far bank if you are on the shallow side of the river. Whether dropping the fly to a rising fish or merely covering likely places, try and ensure it lands about a yard above the desired spot. If drag is no problem, the slight disturbance of the fly alighting this far upstream of a trout will not alarm it. If you must fish almost directly upstream, it may be necessary to drop the fly much closer to the trout for fear of showing too much of the cast.

The strength of your cast must vary according to conditions and the size of fly in use. Naturally, if you fish a mayfly in a weedy river known for its large trout you will select 5lb strength in preference to 3lb. I do not use anything over 3lb on average rivers, often go much lighter for small, shy fish.

As to flies, they are legion! My box contains, in addition to the odd Greenwell tied for surface fishing, the following:

Pheasant Tail
Blue Upright
Iron Blue
Tup's Indispensable
Red Tag
Palmer
Alder
Black Gnat

As a rough guide, use the first three listed early in the season and the others during summer. It's near enough correct to say that river flies are mainly dark and sober in colour in March, April and early May; then they become much showier and daintier, too. Fly sizes ought to vary from 12 (Redditch scale) down to the tiny 17, with sizes 14 and 15 the most useful.

Larger sizes are often desirable in rough water if your eyesight isn't up to following the rough-and-tumble progress of a 17; and

Trout and bridges go together, but it's often more fun to be a spectator on the bridge above rather than a harassed angler trying to switch his fly under a low arch

This trout is being handled very gently before its return to water

that same 17 or even an 18 may be the only thing some over-particular, smutting trout will look at on a sweltering August day.

Smuts, midges and fishermen's curses are best defined as any fly you and I can't possibly spot or imitate, while trout plainly find them adorable. Yes, 'curse' is a grand name for the infinitesimal brutes!

Casting surface fly, as already indicated, isn't quite like the leisurely business of downstream fishing. The longer your cast, the more line you will have to gather with your free hand in order to keep in touch with the fly. On a swift river, this means pulling line back through the rod rings almost as fast as possible, letting the coils lie at your feet. In steadier rivers, you may coil it in your palm or collect it in circles a foot at a time. It pays to *hold* spare line rather than drop it down with the obvious risks of damaging it by treading on it, or perhaps losing a fish because it has become tangled.

Repeating a cast cannot be achieved with one flowing movement as if you were downstream fishing. The line must be lengthened out by a series of false casts—not too many, mind—the first of which should be deliberately off target to allow droplets of water from fly, cast and line to scatter harmlessly below your fish. Subsequent false casts help to dry the fly completely and the last should be on target but a foot or two short; again to avoid scaring the fish.

Some flies float with scarcely any attention at all. A Blue Upright, for instance, with its quill body and sparkling old game cock hackle (ideally) would survive where a Dreadnought might founder! But a Pheasant Tail with its gold wire ribbed body of that material is rather more difficult to keep afloat.

As always, you will try and improve on nature by squirting the fly with a flotant solution or touching up its hackles and body with a hint of line grease. Incidentally, my last tin of line grease was bought just before silk lines virtually went out. I don't need it at all for today's plastic floater lines. But take care not to grease your nylon cast. I've caught scores of trout with a floating cast, but it's better to have it sunk in the surface film where it's less obvious to fish.

Once a fly is soaked it should be squeezed in a pad of amadou, an absorbent fungus which dries and cleans any fly in a couple of seconds. The fly is then ready for a repeat dose of flotant. Never be put off using a fly because of its chewed-up and well-used appearance. When a fly gets that way it's all the more obvious it is worth offering to the trout!

Advice on how to strike a trout which takes your surface fly can only be in general terms—for the speed at which they rise and mouth the fly varies from river to river, and also according to the size of the fish in a particular river. In brooks, hill streams and moorland rivers, you cannot hit your trout quickly enough. In a lowland water of steady flow you may prick half a dozen fish before disciplining yourself to count 'One, Two and Lift', so hooking the next half-dozen. Experience, of course, helps but you would be an extraordinary beginner if you struck trout *too* quickly in your first season.

Reel in slack line while playing a trout, keeping firmly in touch with him *all* the time. If the fish is large he may save you some fuss by first running out the slack from your free hand. Otherwise you must gently pin the trout's end of the line to the rod with your rod-holding hand—not as difficult as it sounds—and hastily reel up the slack line.

Now, for an outdoor approach to these mysteries, let's go to the Welsh border and that splendid stream, the lower Monnow, on a pleasant May morning.

PRACTICE

The Monnow is the sort of small river on which I've never had an unhappy day. Here it runs through pleasant, open countryside some miles downstream of the Black Mountains where it rises. The Welsh borderland is a haven for trout anglers; its streams and the hills which produce them are alike delightful.

It is the third week of May. A benign, warm spell has lasted over a week and looks like continuing. Hear the cuckoo? While you can hear his call you are fishing the cream of the trout season. There's an odd saying on the Devon Exe that the cuckoo calls the salmon over a certain weir. Probably this saying is common to other rivers. It boils down to this: once the cuckoo is about in numbers the higher air and water temperatures of late spring have arrived. Fly fishing weather de-luxe!

These Border trout are three or four to the pound in the hills; but on this stretch of river I'm hoping those you catch will average 6oz, with one or two in the bag double that weight. Be optimistic about it. If you go out expecting a duck you aren't likely to make a century!

Three things make this period of May an interesting and satisfying one for the fly fisherman. First, trout can be expected to surface feed during most of the day; secondly, there isn't likely to be a great evening rise; finally, you are just ahead of the mayfly which, despite its name, does not normally appear in force on our rivers until the first fortnight in June. More about the mayfly later.

It's an ideal morning; a certain amount of cloud, scarcely any wind, the river sparkling. I'll gillie for you until midday, after which the pull of the river will probably be too much for me.

Take my advice and shorten that allegedly 9ft cast you've tied on. You can see for yourself you overestimated when making it up and it's a foot longer than the rod. Leave the fly end alone: snip 2ft 6in from the heavy portion at the top and then tie a new loop to re-join it to the line. The reason is simply that you can bring a hooked fish closer to you without reeling the line and cast knot through the top ring of the rod—always an unwise move if you are handling a big trout—and casting the fly is easier with a shorter cast. I don't think a full 9ft cast gives any advantage on a little river of this kind, constantly broken up by rocks, dividing itself around small islands and in places overhung by trees.

It's a bright day so we'll start you off with a light-bodied Blue Upright size 14 for the rough water just above the bridge. Here the river is penned in by rock walls and it has to hurry along. No need to wade, but you would be well advised to keep on your knees for the first twenty yards—it's not too uncomfortable in thigh waders.

You can see for yourself there's no room for long casting here. The river isn't much wider than your dining room. Creep down the steep bank and out over the rock formation, taking care not to slip or make scraping noises with the hobs in your waders. Down on your knees, now, and pull off a yard of line. Flick the fly up and across, pull another yard off the reel and repeat the process. One more yard of line and that will be enough. Surprising how *difficult* it is to cast so short a line.

Try a cast almost directly upstream first, where the water only looks about six inches deep. Actually it's twice that depth and every so often you'll find a trout will come out of the deeper water to take the fly. Next cast must be a foot or two further across the current; and so on, until all the available water has been covered. It doesn't do any harm in such fast water to fish over each particular 'line' of fly travel several times. For a variety of reasons the trout may not come up first time.

Again, I must emphasise that you can overdo thoroughness; give the trout up to half a dozen casts in one spot and if they disappoint you, move on.

And moving on, in these circumstances, means shuffling painfully forward a yard or two on your knees.

Keep casting, giving an extra flick every so often to dry the fly properly. You are 'fishing the water' because nothing is visibly rising yet; but I know the trout are here and . . . yes . . . good thing that one grabbed the fly the moment it dropped on the water: you were able to strike and make contact instantly without slack line trouble.

Try and work him in under your rod tip in the relatively shallow, slack water. No good—he's rushed off downstream in the main current and nothing strains a hookhold more than trying to pull a fish back. If he was completely beaten you might slide him upstream over the top of the 'waves' in the roughest stream. This one, although only a quarter pound or so, is not beaten but tugging actively. Normally I should say move downstream level with him to finish the business or, if you cared to risk a loss, play him out and pull him back up. This time I'll save you the decision by netting him myself.

See! Hooked by a fragment of badly torn skin on the edge of his lower jaw. Another twist and turn and he might have been gone. I've knocked him on the head since he is a fat quarter-pounder, though usually I prefer to return such fish to reach their average on rivers like this.

By the way, apart from any rules about size limits and total bags made by owners or associations controlling rivers, it's useful to remember that river authorities and others issuing licences normally stipulate a minimum length at which trout can be killed. Often this is as low as 7in. When you recall that an average 9in trout weighs only 5oz it's obvious such a limit is not high enough.

I'm surprised you didn't pick up another trout or two in the fast water. My fault, perhaps, for thrusting you into it straightway. You weren't too happy with the speed of the fly. So let's walk quietly through these mossy old boulders at the side of the river and try the next good stretch of water flowing gently beneath a line of alder trees.

You will need to wade here in order to make room for your back cast, for there are trees on both banks. About a third of the way across will do, just over knee deep. The far bank is attractive to trout, not only because of the trees but by reason of the numerous stones and boulders underwater. An ideal hidey-hole situation.

You are wading in very cautiously, I'm glad to see, and looking where your feet are going, which is always wise. While you are moving about on *any* river bed there's no time to gaze at the birds, or even the fish.

Now you are in position, but don't unhitch the fly for a moment. Instead, study the current and the layout of the tree branches in front and behind, and watch for rising trout.

At a conservative estimate I'd say there were half-a-dozen feeding and catchable trout in this dozen yards of water. Some are not much beyond midstream—the smaller ones—and others are among the rocks and tucked close in beneath the far bank.

Those gentle rings in the water like raindrops are all trout. The surface is broken by one every twenty seconds. At this point a scientifically-minded angler would produce a small muslin net and catch whatever nymphs or duns were coming down river before deciding what fly to employ. There might be some justification for proceeding thus slowly on a chalk stream, but I'll guarantee most of these Border trout will have a go at your floating fly even if they are mainly taking nymphs.

Did you see that rise, two rod lengths upstream of you and three yards further across? That's your closest feeding trout apparently, so try him first. Remember, it's better to be a little wide or short at the first attempt than to slap half the cast or even some line across the fish's 'window'.

That's something else I ought to explain. By 'window' I mean the area which a trout can see from his position in the river; it includes the surface over which flies are drifting and a substantial area above water, too. I'm no scientist, so I treat the trout as if they had eyes in their tails and catch my share. Suffice it to say that anglers of scientific bent have worked out just what a trout at a given depth of water can see. By wading, as you are, and keeping quiet, you will not disturb these trout upstream. And when they are preoccupied with their feeding in this way they seem to lose some of their normal wariness. If you stumble or make a splashy cast they may not take much notice.

I see trout number one liked the fly, he sucked it in quietly while you were fiddling with the line coils in your hand. You wondered why the fly appeared to have sunk? Moral—never take your eyes off it, then you'll find out.

Number two has risen several times over that attractive patch of golden gravel in the main current. If we were on the other bank looking down at him we should see a fat little trout swinging about in the current six or twelve inches below the surface, taking an interest in everything going by. Sometimes he would move forward and upward to meet surface flies, sometimes taking them and dropping gently back, sometimes following them for a foot or more before sucking them in daintily. Such an inspection of the angler's fly is always nerve-racking when it can be watched!

Try and shake a hint of slack line as you finish your cast. This trout is lying just beyond the main force of the current.

That was a good cast, the fly coming down to him smoothly, glinting attractively, no sign of drag. He's got it with a small splash, you struck decisively and not *too* hastily—this is close-range fishing in steady water—and now the rod tip is bucking as he thumps down towards the safety of his home among the rocks. The rule is to keep him from flying upstream and disturbing other rising trout. Don't hesitate to bring the rod point down to water level on either side of you to turn him if he shows signs of going up : but *never* point the rod at a fish, always maintain a safe curve in it.

Your fish is now well beaten and floundering. Time to net him, drawing him over the meshes with a firm pull. Second blood of the day, a nice half-pounder.

The preliminary struggles of number two must have affected number three's appetite temporarily. He hasn't shown up again. Let's forget him and go for number four which rose just off the roots of that alder a moment ago. You'll need a couple more yards of line and, I think, a step upstream to cover him. Move yourself first before drying and re-greasing the fly. It's useful to have both hands clear for such jobs, so stick the butt of your rod into one of your waders where it will balance handily.

Now for number four! That cast was about a foot short and six inches this side of him. Sometimes they will charge a yard across at a fly, but it's better to be accurate. Try again. A couple of false casts and . . . you've hitched the fly on one of the trees behind, a common enough happening. Don't try snatching it back. It might come loose, or you might only lose the fly; but rod tips have been broken in this way. Point the rod tip up the line and give a gentle drawing pull. If the fly holds firm you would normally leave the river and attend to it. In this case I know I can retrieve it for you. But take the hint from that back cast and wade a little deeper and further upstream.

Back on the job again, and at once you're into another first-timer, with a great flounce as he turned on the fly. It fell rather close to his nose and instinctively he grabbed. Equally instinctively he went straight down into that network of alder roots and broke you. They were his nearest cover—too near for your comfort I'm afraid. The drill with such trout is to strike and haul hard downstream all in one movement. You can do it with half-pounders and get away with it.

Never mind, I assure you he *was* only a half-pounder. I've been broken in just the same way by even smaller fish in some snag-ridden brooks. Tie on another Blue Upright, same size, and try for the remaining brace. Both of them are feeding close to the far bank several yards further upstream.

Number five certainly looks catchable. He has been feeding

steadily, showing his head and tail frequently on his journeys to the surface. He looks quite a good size. The snag with this one is that large, rounded rock just upstream of him. It divides the current and sets up some little eddies which may result in drag on your fly. Try a cast and see what happens.

Yes, I feared as much. The top half of your cast seemed to pause as if by magic over the rock, swinging the finer point and fly round across the surface in a most unnatural way. You will have to try and achieve some slack in the final feet of your cast. Give the rod tip a good waggle this time. Ah, that was lucky and unlucky. A momentary puff of wind came just as you cast, and unwittingly you took advantage of it. He rose quietly and for some reason your strike merely scraped him.

He may not have been greatly alarmed, but it's not worth waiting to see if he'll rise again. Once, when fishing a crystal clear Austrian mountain river, I located a trout of about a pound feeding in a fast run and hooked, or rather scraped him twice. Yet he came again and was landed. That was a decidedly bold or daft trout!

Now it's time for number six, but before you start casting take a look at your nylon. See anything? Those two little knots near the fly have tied themselves while you've been casting. They are called wind knots and they reduce the breaking strain of the cast considerably. I never continue fishing with them, either undoing them if they are very loose or cutting them out and joining the cast with a blood knot.

Number six is about as many inches from the far bank, so your cast will be a fairly long one, though straightforward. Odd, he must have seen the fly that time. Try a couple more casts, however, before pausing to think. Still no good?

You must ask yourself whether the fly or its presentation was at fault. There! He rose again so you haven't frightened the trout.

Is it to be a different size fly or a changed pattern? Not size, I think. In salmon fishing, we rate sizes more important than patterns; with trout it's a good thing to show them something different. Put on one of my favourite, bushy Pheasant Tails. This is a darker fly with a heavier, 'meaty' body. Border trout love it.

Yet it hasn't done any good. Over his head half a dozen times without response and the beggar's *still* rising. Under conditions like these it would be foolish to go on swopping surface fly patterns in the hope of finding the one to attract him. That trout, though he appears to be feeding on top, is too busy taking nymphs to bother with a single floating fly.

The Pheasant Tail makes a very good nymph imitation (properly tied). But rather than change flies again we'll just try an old dodge on this character. Spit on your fly, give it a thoroughly good dousing in the river, anything to ensure it will sink as soon as you've cast.

You should see a movement in the water if he takes, your cast will draw under too. . . . Splendid! He had it first time and you made contact perfectly. A couple of good runs, a jump . . . oh, and he's off. Never mind. The important thing is that you persuaded him to take—you won the battle of wits. Remember the 'nymph' tip: it will collect you a lot of trout over the years.

Now how about an early lunch?

The tail of this pool—I call it the Long Pool because it's one of the biggest and longest I know on the Monnow—is an ideal place to lunch and see the odd small fry rising. You will see one or two grayling, I've no doubt. They are spawning about now, but they still find time to bob up to the fly occasionally. Some so-called anglers are uncivilised enough to knock them on the head out of season because they consider them a menace in a trout stream. This is a silly attitude, particularly in rivers where the grayling is indigenous. They are handsome, excellent sporting fish which extend our fly-rod season by several months.

Now I'll leave you to your own devices for a while and go upstream to see if I can catch something. Why not try the top half of this pool, right up as far as that overhanging bramble bush? It ought to be good for another brace of trout. Don't bother your head over those midstream rises we've been watching, honestly they are only grayling. I'll leave the next couple of hundred yards of water untouched for you. The next meadow up is quite open and easy for casting.

* * *

Well, here we are again and what have you been up to? Lost a really big one, did you? One of those midstream risers in the

Long Pool, was it? Well, it possibly could have been a trout though I'm prepared to bet it wasn't.

Went up and down the pool making a mighty wave, pulling the rod tip right over. Yes. Then started tugging and tugging towards the far bank, went downstream and kept on going. What did you do? Hung on like grim death! Then the cast came back without the fly and there was a tremendous swirl in the fast shallows and the 'trout' vanished. Oh yes, it was a grayling and one of the bigger ones of the river, I expect. Bad luck, but it served you right for meddling with her ladyship at spawning time!

Just above us there's rather an interesting stretch of water, completely overhung by trees and full of rocks which break up the current and provide plenty of good trout lies. It's only possible to wade it from the left bank from below to begin with, though after a few yards the going gets easier and shallower. Would you care to sit and watch me try it?

Down the bank I go, sliding as quietly as possible almost to the tops of my waders. This is the sort of place that must be learned by trial and error—and many a bootful of water. However, I soon learned this way in after watching the trout moving among the boulders and under the trees. There were so many of them when I first explored this stretch of river that I knew they simply *had* to be tackled.

I am right-handed and not ambidextrous. If I was, the first few casts would be made left-handed here, back up under my own bank. Remember, we are on the left bank. Fortunately a few short casts can be made back-handed just as easily. There's no possibility of lifting the rod tip to cast in the normal overhead manner. The fly has to be wheedled out to the fish. I've pulled a couple of yards of line off the reel, so here goes. Notice the rod tip stayed about a foot above water level all the time and I didn't move it much more than a yard forward and back. It was enough to get the fly out. Again, and the fly shoots slightly better towards our bank.

Got him! One advantage of this close-range fishing is the control you have over the fish with the rod tip almost on top of him; and there isn't too much current here. An average trout, that, bringing my total to two and a half brace (ie, five).

Now I've cast a foot too far up and thrown the Pheasant Tail right over that sycamore branch. If I can pull it back very carefully we might see some fun: there are two trout rising in that very spot, dead level. Good, it's drawing over. It's dropped beautifully and one of those twins has nabbed it, evidently thinking it a succulent morsel falling from the tree. Trees, bushes, even beds of rushes at the river's edge are *always* valuable. A grand fighter, that trout, and at 14oz I shan't catch a better one today.

Once I've moved a couple of painful steps upstream I shall be able to step a pace away from the bank and try for that trout on the other side which is rising so busily. I shall just have room to switch the cast behind me and then propel it across with a decisive wrist and forearm action. You'll find with practice you can automatically select the best cast to reach a trout in a difficult spot. Sometimes when really cramped you can hold the fly between finger and thumb and catapult it to a fish, using the bend of the rod tip to achieve the necessary momentum.

Ah, that trout was so hungry he didn't mind a splashy and wildly inaccurate cast. Freedom for him, I've taken as many trout as I need today. I never understand why anglers feel they must kill every sizeable trout they catch, unless it's a rule of the water. See how easily I freed the hook from that fellow while he was still under water?

The next few steps have taken me to the ideal place on a river this size overhung by trees—midstream. From here, wading becomes progressively easier and I can cast to either bank, covering any rising fish. Most of the time I am not lifting the rod overhead, although there is room in places, but sweeping it to and fro sideways and at waist level. This cast is not quite as accurate as the overhead version, but it is a most necessary variation.

You'll have noticed, I hope, how I keep moving and the speed at which I fish the surface fly upstream. I'm a firm believer in frequent casts over plenty of water, even where rising trout have not been located. I don't think one should hammer the fly over an individual trout. If you spot a large one it's better to sit and watch for him to come on the feed, and cast seldom.

Some anglers would be happy with 200 yards of this river on such a day, and still leave part of it unfished. Others might just as easily fish their way up two miles of water. I suspect their bags would weigh much the same at the end of the day, but the short-distance man would probably have fewer though better trout to show for his patience. It all boils down to temperament again.

We've got another two hours' sunshine and fishing time yet. Around seven o'clock it will become cool and most of the fish will have disappeared for the night—a hint to us to do the same.

But there's no mistaking a true evening rise. Every fish in the river seems to be on the move, becoming bolder in the dusk and yet often quite tetchy about the fly. The only certain factor about an evening rise is the time you will finish—when it's too dark to see the fly. It can be one of the most fascinating things in fishing, and one of the most frustrating. Later, I shall try and introduce you to its pains and pleasures.

CHAPTER THREE

TROUT: *Big River—Sunk Fly*

THEORY

FRANKLY there isn't much difference in fishing small and big rivers except the obvious, physical one. I look upon rivers such as the Wye, the lower Usk, the Tweed or Tay, as the big rivers of this country. Rather surprisingly, such rivers do not on average produce larger trout. True, their pools hold a proportion of tough old stagers weighing several pounds, but so do most rivers. Such fish are virtually never taken on fly—they are the province of the minnow and worm anglers.

Obviously your first thought on reaching the banks of a big river is 'Where shall I find the trout?' and the answer is, briefly, in all the places you would expect them on rivers of more moderate scale. Think of a big river as your small river scaled up four or five times.

The pools will contain a proportion of fish, so will the shallows and the fast water between pools; but it's a good general rule to by-pass places of too great or too little depth during the day; on summer nights some shallows offer great sport.

Look for the glides in the big river to find the trout. Stretches of water varying from two to six feet in depth where the current is steady are promising. Select a stretch of water where trout are rising—or expected to rise—and treat it as if it was a separate entity. Concentrate on a particular stretch which you can fish properly and don't try and cover the whole of the river. Imagine trying to wade up the middle of a river the size of the Wye at Hay, casting a small fly to right and left and searching all the water in the way I suggested in the last section! It cannot be done, and should not even be attempted.

In some circumstances a big river might demand heavier tackle than your 9ft rod. Many northerners would ask for another 18in rod length to cover the wide flats of Tweed or Tay. But most of our big rivers, except in times of flood when they are not fishable with fly, are never in too great a hurry to reach the sea and the normal outfit will suffice. If you go in for much fishing of this type I suspect you will stick to the 9ft rod for summer fishing with the floating fly, but acquire a longer, softer-actioned rod for fishing the sunk lure early and late in the year. Such a rod, heavier though it may be, is at the same time more restful when casting a longer line.

So I suggest a careful look at your big river when you finally reach it, and a chat with some local anglers who can tell you the hopeful places and the places which inevitably disappoint. It doesn't take long to discover this for yourself on a small river. You can learn a mile of water quite well in a week. On the big river, you might waste almost a week coming to the right conclusions.

If you are going to fish sunk fly you are certain to be wading from the shallow side of the river. You will be well clear of obstructions and should have no difficulty in fishing a trio of flies, each spaced some 18in to two feet apart on your nine or even ten foot cast. Never ignore local suggestions as to patterns. The drill for downstream sunk fly fishing is exactly the same as that suggested in the small river section. You will find yourself wading deeper and throwing a longer line, but otherwise adopting the same tactics.

I'm going to wean you away from downstream fishing, however, and introduce you to the rather more difficult but infinitely more satisfying medium of fishing the sunk fly upstream. Two flies are enough on a cast for this work and they should not be too large. They should be tied rather sparsely and be capable of sinking instantly on reaching the water. To assist sinking, some anglers like to rib them with heavy wire. Do remember, though, that the trout will be looking forwards and upwards when they are on the feed and it's silly to sink your flies a yard when a few inches would be ample.

Downstream fishing is a long-range business, but when casting a sunk fly across and upstream I like to be reasonably close to the fish. You cannot fail to see a rise to your fly when it is sitting on the surface. It is the easiest thing in the world, however, to miss a trout taking your fly only an inch or two underneath the surface.

In this form of fishing you are watching not only for the splash or movement of the trout in the water, but the dull glint of his sides as he takes well down, or the slight movement of line or cast when he takes. You will not feel tugs on your rod tip, as in downstream fishing, because the fly or flies always move back towards your position on a slack line. As in surface fly fishing, you must keep constantly in touch with your fly without causing it to accelerate or drag in an unnatural way; and if you are using two flies it pays to lift the rod tip steadily, bringing the dropper to the surface as the cast fishes out.

The faster the water the more difficult putting this artistic method of fishing into practice becomes. Choose a place where the river's flow is not too wild to begin operations. If you are wading deep in rough water, you may find it necessary to cast almost directly upstream to avoid undue drag.

Say you are fishing two flies. As they drop gently under, start retrieving line with your free hand until you judge the total line and cast length left out is about one and a half times as long as the rod. At this juncture, cease drawing line and begin lifting the rod point, fishing the flies in slight jerks and eventually lifting the dropper to the surface in the manner of a nymph hatching. How much movement you give the flies depends on you—and the trout. Sometimes they prefer them just drifting, sometimes they will snatch at a fly being drawn steadily and smoothly through the water. Movement indicates underwater life—and food—to a trout. A sunk fly drifting inertly down the current may not.

Having lifted the flies and got the rod tip almost up to vertical, a backwards flick should start the false cast which will take out the gathered line from your free hand, and away upstream goes your next cast. Any indication of a take should be answered by an instant strike. It is better to strike on suspicion and meet empty air a few times than to wait for a positive sign of a trout. Some anglers watch the place where they believe their flies to be. Others keep an eye on the upper part of their cast and strike the moment it stops or draws against the stream. The second method is the obvious one for you unless you have exceptional eyesight *and* second sight! But, I repeat, do respond instantly to any indication the cast gives. Trout can grab and reject a fly all in a split second.

But enough of theory! Let us be off to our next river, the Breconshire Usk, to get those flies into the water and see how the method works in practice.

PRACTICE

We have had days out in March and May, so for the sake of example here we are on the banks of the Usk in mid-April; a good month for the sunk fly and a good river for the method.

Step cautiously down the steep bank. Notice that rising fish only a yard or two out. It might be a dace but it is much more likely to be a trout. There have been showers for the past week and the river is tinged with colour. You will be in and out of your oilskins today, but there will be warmth in the intervals of sunshine.

The Usk is a river once famed for its fly life and great rises. Old hands condemn the march of civilisation which, they claim, has reduced the fly markedly in the past half-century. You and I are in no position to dispute this. We can only judge the river as we find it: full of trout which at times rise very freely indeed. There can be long periods of inactivity, but when the trout *do* come on sport can be fast and furious!

You have a cast ready, I see, but the 2in dropper link is too short. This makes tying on new flies a tricky business since the nylon shortens a little each time. And I like the dropper to fall well away from the main cast when it is finally worked to the surface. Under the water it's bound to be fairly close to the cast but when you lift it at the end of its journey downstream I like to think a trout will see very little cast indeed: just a tiny nymph-like object moving naturally and attractively upwards.

Therefore make your dropper link four or five inches long and risk a few extra tangles when casting. Droppers always do try and knot themselves around the parent cast, which is why so many anglers fish single fly. On the other hand, I'm sure a

Angler versus trout on the lovely River Usk

Rainbow trout are usually the strongest fighters of all. Here a pounder is netted from a private lake

dropper substantially adds to your chances of catching average fish.

Your 9ft rod will do. Steel yourself not to look at any rises beyond the middle of the river because you could not reach them, and because there is more than enough water for a day's fishing in the half you can cover.

While you have been tackling up I've seen several more rising fish within easy reach of this bank (the right bank) and, as there is just room to squeeze along without going into the shallows, I suggest you work towards that ruined old willow about fifty yards upstream. The water is slightly coloured and the bank provides a good background to conceal you so you can stoop and fish in relative comfort instead of having to creep and crawl as you did on the Monnow.

I suggest you first get into position and then knot on your flies. Any slight disturbance you make going down that crumbly bank will be forgotten in the time it takes you to tie them on. Select a March Brown as tail fly and try an Iron Blue Nymph for the dropper. The Usk produces natural flies of both types, so there's no sense in putting up blatant fancy patterns to start the day.

A fancy fly is simply a tying which is not meant to be a direct imitation or representation of the natural. The trout almost always take them equally well—to the great grief of angler-entomologists—but there are occasions on rivers such as this when you must get as close as possible to the natural for the very best results. You cannot shut your eyes to the fact that trout occasionally become *very* selective in their choice of natural fly and extraordinarily choosy about the artificial.

Most trout are caught while a rise is coming on, and again when it is tapering off, and not at its height. This is worth bearing in mind when you are floundering about in the midst of a hundred madly rising trout, offering them a dozen beautiful flies one after the other and being consistently refused.

Strip off some line and begin fishing. Don't try casting too far : ten or twelve yards is sufficient. Draw the line constantly to keep in touch, then begin lifting the rod and working the flies very gently. The sketch overleaf shows just about the right angle.

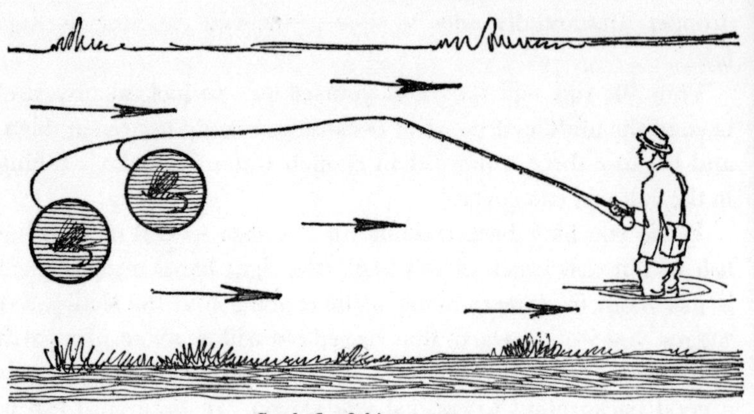

Sunk fly fishing upstream

Remember, most nymphs do not make exaggerated movements underwater, though some undoubtedly move fast. Be on your guard for a fish as those flies start lifting at the end of the cast. You may well be startled by the sudden dash and grab of a trout. Even if your rod tip is nearly vertical, a wrist movement should hook this sort of taker. There! A quiet little swirl in the water where I judge your tail fly was. There was no movement of the cast but I expect that fish touched the fly and you ought to have struck. Keep your eyes skinned. Fly fishing is easy—catching trout demands a little more from you!

A trout has just moved fifteen yards upstream of you and a mere seven or eight yards out. You saw him? Good. Don't hurry to reach him, be content to mark the spot mentally and drop the flies extra softly when you reach it. It isn't always easy to pinpoint a rise away from the banks in a river this size, and the trout may be cruising about anyway when there is some extra water and colour in the river, but you can get an approximate idea where each rising fish is. If I see a rise at a distance I try and pinpoint it against some landmark such as a tree branch, a clump of thistles or even a tuft of grass. Try and be accurate with your first cast when stalking trout.

I believe your next cast will be over the fish. Yes. Swirling rise and strike were almost simultaneous. You timed the strike correctly because you were keyed up and expecting some fun. That's how you should be *all* the time if you want to become one of

England's greatest fly fishermen! No need to shout for the net in such anguished tones. It will be perfectly easy to beach your trout there. Play him to a standstill on top of the water and then draw him gently ashore. If he does start flapping in the shallows, allow him to calm down and then continue to persuade him ashore.

This fish took your tail fly, which left the dropper up the cast and out of harm's way as you beached him. In theory, you can get into trouble when beaching a fish on the dropper because the tail fly may get hooked up in a stone or weed. To my mind it's still preferable to netting fish when two or more flies are in use.

Your trout weighs 9oz and he's now in the bag. Don't waste time. When you've finished with this length you will go over it again, wading to cover further across the river.

Another one hooked! This time on the dropper, as you were lifting it. And his immediate response was a wild, downwards plunge which certainly helped to clear all the slack line in your free hand. Everything's gone dead? Don't pull too hard for a moment. Probably he has weeded you. There are occasional hefty clumps of weed in rivers like this and if trout can reach them they dive in.

Still no movement? Relax all strain on the fish for a moment, drop downstream a few paces and try a pull from a different angle. Still no good? Your trout may be gripping the weed stems in his mouth, or he may have turned a couple of circles in the weed and so taken the cast around it. The longer he stays there the less likely you are to bag him—so try handlining.

Point the rod tip down along your line and pull very gently. Nylon is a tough material, it is stretchy and capable of cutting through substantial weed fronds. A slight pull from the hand is stronger than anything the rod tip can give. The moment you feel an answering wriggle from the weeds, up with the rod and play the fish away from them. Good. It worked. And that's your brace. He weighs the same as the first. Check your cast for any signs of damage as a result of the weeding and see there are no extra knots in it.

Now you're approaching the old willow. Deeper water and two or three fish rising alongside it. I'm afraid it will mean casting almost directly upstream for it's too deep to wade out and throw the flies back across to the trout. I suggest your chances will be improved if you cut off the dropper and allow the tail fly on its finer length of cast to drop unimpeded on their respective noses. It will be exactly like surface fly fishing, casting to known rising trout and watching for a take. I should work up reasonably close to the lowest of these fish: say two rod lengths. You had better creep along on your knees. The nearer you are, the better your chances of hooking them.

You delivered the fly with a 'bang' but the first was still hungry enough to want it. Perhaps he thought it was a baby sparrow doing a crash dive—he couldn't have mistaken it for a March Brown! Six ounces, that foolish fish.

The next trout was equally hungry, I see. Ah, he's off! Examine your fly. Half the hook gone? No, it's not in the trout's jaw. I expect it touched a stone or tree branch in one of your back casts. Very often you break a hook point that way and never feel a thing. What remained was enough to jam against the trout's jaw momentarily.

Never mind, tie on a replacement March Brown and tell yourself you'll catch an even better one.

And so you have! A good 11oz fish to boost the average a little.

I can see quite a number of trout moving on the flat you've just fished up. There's every indication of a surface rise in the offing, so why not fish it up again, this time wading and aiming at the rises?

Leave the March Brown on as your tail fly and tie on a Gold Ribbed Hare's Ear as dropper, giving it a touch of grease to float it. You will be offering the trout a choice of March Brown nymph and hatching Olive, which the Hare's Ear is thought to represent. If a trout takes the nymph, the surface fly sometimes acts as a float and gives you a splendid indication—and of course you'll be in no doubt when your surface fly is sucked down.

I don't need to point out rising fish. You can see for yourself the dimples all across the river. Between a dozen and a score of trout must be feeding within your range at the moment, with more likely to show up soon. Wade in and start covering them.

How long have you been fishing without a touch? I should

say less than ten minutes and I think the blame is partly yours. With so many trout popping up you are getting much too excited and trying to cover them too quickly. Once or twice you have hit your rod tip with the flies on your forward cast and become fearfully tangled up, just because you changed your mind where to aim the cast at the last moment.

Concentrate on one rising fish, giving him half a dozen careful casts at regular intervals instead of slamming the flies down on his head twice and then covering another fish. Tell yourself trout don't fear drag any less when they are rising everywhere in sight. Every individual riser is a problem to be solved.

Now, I must admit, you have been refused too often for it to be entirely your fault. Let's have the Hare's Ear off and substitute your former pattern which caught a fish, the Iron Blue; this time a floating pattern.

It worked: so there's an example of selective feeding on the part of the trout and the success wrought by the right fly pattern. Now you have a second trout and the fun looks like becoming fast and furious. Swing your cast in to me quickly and I'll tie on a second Iron Blue, a nymph, in place of the March Brown tail fly. *Always* give the trout what they've clearly shown they want.

There. You have had an hour of the sort of sport the Usk provides on occasions. Seven trout netted and another half-dozen risen, pricked or lost in play. And that seems to be the end of the rise. The glorious hour of the Iron Blue is over, although one had better stay on the cast in case of any interested stragglers.

Lunch is now indicated; afterwards you can flog away trying for your last trout to make the total six brace. Oilskins are indicated, too. Who knows, the storm may have affected the rise of trout and stopped them prematurely. Certainly most of them went down (ie ceased rising) in the space of ten minutes or less. More likely, however, their fly food supply lessened suddenly. Fly hatches can be of very short duration.

When you first saw this beat you bemoaned the lack of faster water. Well, there is one place where a good current runs down even on this shallow side of the river. Above the old willow at the very top of our water there is a concrete groyne built to improve the salmon fishing and it juts out enough to cause extra current.

There I hope you'll pick up your twelfth trout of a successful day.

Look there! A rise just a few yards downstream near the willow's lowest branch. Cheeky fish! Heave the flies over him for fun. You've got him—he had the dropper instantly and hooked himself on the tight line. He's not a trout, though, but a lively dace. You *have* managed to catch a dozen fish in the day!

Put him back carefully. I know dace are considered vermin in this and other trout rivers, but killing them in ones and twos isn't going to make the slightest difference to the trout stock, and it is the coarse fish close season. Besides, there are times when a shoal of dace will provide some entertainment on an otherwise blank day.

CHAPTER FOUR

TROUT: *Big River–Surface Fly*

THEORY

EVERYTHING I said about surface fly fishing on a small river applies equally to the big river. Adopt the same principles. I do repeat, however, the necessity for not trying to cover too much of the big river's acres of water.

In this section we are going to deal with one particular aspect of surface fishing—the evening rise. A big, open river, full of trout, is a splendid sight at dusk on a summer evening, with fish showing all over the place where none moved for hours during the day. The later it gets, the better your chance of a big fish until darkness snuffs out everything, forcing you to change to a big sunk fly if you insist on continuing.

Evening rises are always best during warm, settled weather. The months of June, July and August are pre-eminent, though you may meet a good rise in May or September if the evening air temperature doesn't drop too sharply. On the rivers and lakes of this country you will catch the full evening rise perfectly if you saunter out as the sun is setting. Some trout, normally the smaller fry, will be rising already, but the rise proper will begin when the sun has dropped from sight. Where a hill or even a belt of trees causes a premature sunset the rise will start that much earlier.

We are dealing with a big river in this section—but whatever the water you must remember that time to fish is limited. I reckon you have an hour and a half of light at most when the sun drops from view. It is vital to choose one good length of river and stick to it. Starting in one place, changing your mind and half running up a quarter mile of river bank to have a few wild casts and then rushing back to your original starting point is sheer idiocy at this time of day. Yet I've done it—though I am wiser now—and others I've seen still do it.

Naturally, as the light goes, it becomes increasingly difficult to see what fly the trout are taking. It's fair to say that on most rivers they will vary their diet and accept your offering without too much investigation. In general terms, any bushy-looking fly will be taken as a sedge in the evening; and a tiny Black Gnat, for example, will continue to do well, representing the multitude of midges and smuts which buzz about over the water especially on hot, damp evenings.

A third type of natural fly may force you to alter your campaign occasionally even on rivers other than chalk streams. That is the so-called spinner, which is the last stage of the natural. Here it is:

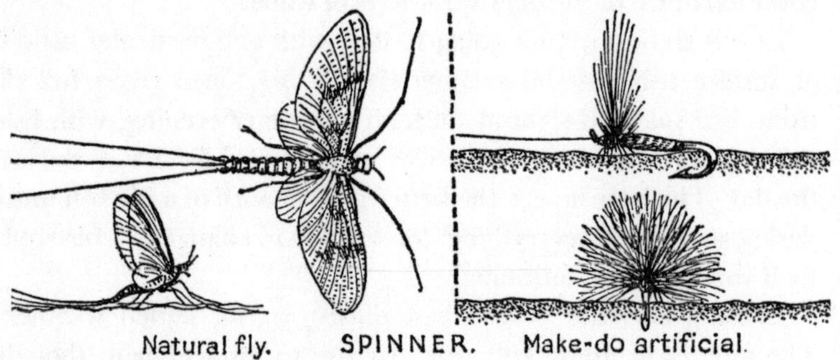

The spinner—and how to create a makeshift artificial

Earlier in the day you may have cast a surface fly dressed to represent a dun. This means the natural after hatching but before taking off from the river surface. When it has mated and shed its eggs, the little fly finally falls on the river again, wings stretched out flat this time instead of being perkily cocked, to be taken by the knowing, waiting trout.

Flies are tied specifically to represent spinners but you needn't worry too much about these patterns. Take your scissors to a Blue Upright and cut the underpart of its hackle as shown above (right) making it lie flat on the surface film like the natural.

By June, when the evening rise is getting under way, trout will be in all the fast areas of water where the river dashes between rocks and foams from one pool to the next. In the evenings they tend to spread across into shallow water, too, sometimes rising between the wading angler and the shore. One good-sized pool may well be sufficient water for an evening rise. You may decide to fish gradually up the body of the pool in the first hour and concentrate on the fast water at the head of the pool in the last of the light. These are the sort of tactics to adopt.

You may decide to fish a very small fly for the first half-hour—a Black Gnat size 16, for example—replacing it with a size 12 Pheasant Tail for the faster water in the fading light. Rises become harder to see, of course, and you may find yourself striking by 'ear' in the dusk in quiet water. There is always a glimmer of light on the surface when all traces of sunset have gone : you can take advantage of it to watch your fly if you angle yourself accordingly. It pays to identify one riser among a welter of rising fish, and offer the fly to it as if it was the only feeding trout in the river. This strategy will result in more fish for your bag than haphazard casting.

Normally, I do not alter the strength of my cast for the evening rise. If the trout are going to gorge madly and indiscreetly on anything that floats, their carnival time isn't likely to last more than ten minutes or so. Usually they do *not* go mad and a 'ship's hawser' of a cast would put them down almost as quickly as it would in bright sunshine. I do, however, carry a couple of spare casts in case of tangles. The dusk and a splendid rise are no times for quiet contemplation, or reflective tying up of a new cast when all efforts to free the wind knots and tangles in its predecessor have failed. Simply remove the whole knotted cast and replace it with another, complete with fly, coiled on one of those useful little celluloid cast-carriers obtainable at any tackle dealer. If you have to tie on a new fly in the dusk, hold the fly and cast point up against the sky and you will see what you are doing.

One of my spare casts is slightly shorter and stouter than usual. It carries a big bushy Palmer fly which the trout are meant to take for a sedge. The cast, tapering to 5lb b.s., may be put on when it is almost dark, providing some natural sedges are about, scuttling across the river and causing the trout to chase them. When this happens your fly *must* drag for the best results. It is exciting fishing.

PRACTICE

This quiet country lane leads to the River Usk. It is June and it's been a hot day with remarkably few trout moving. But the air is cooler now and the sun has lost its intensity. It is a real pleasure to walk along the lane, climb the gate and skirt around the hayfield to reach the river.

This stretch of river is very different from the first Usk beat you fished. Here the river is narrower. It runs fast down a series of ledges and then pours through a rocky funnel only a dozen yards wide. The main run of current is down the left bank and you will be fishing it in waders from the right bank side. Gradually it widens out into an attractive flat before flowing under the lane bridge and down into a salmon pool.

Trees overhang the fastest water at the head of the pool, and there is a high bank opposite with plenty of undergrowth. One problem is the amount of 'dead' water down your bank. It is absolutely slack and contains very few trout. You must wade, cautiously because it is three to four feet deep, but wade you must to make room for your back cast and to reach out to that main current under the far bank. The closer you can approach it, the less drag there will be on your line from the slack water.

I can see you are eager to start although the sun is still above the trees. Why not tie on a size 16 Tup and see if it interests any of the small fry a hundred yards downstream where the river widens out? I don't think you should start flogging the best of the water for at least another hour. And you'd better attach your net to the fishing bag. You can't beach fish here.

Watch the water under the far bank. Often good trout move only inches away from it, dimpling very quietly. I don't think the midstream risers at present are any great size. And look how the sun glints on your cast! Give it a rub with the Fuller's Earth and glycerine mixture.

Both those rises were salmon parr, I think, and your strike fortunately wasn't quick enough for them. But here's something better. See that cluster of rocks half in the water almost opposite? Something rose a foot below the downstream rock where the current is diverted outwards slightly. If you *can* get the fly over there, dropping it really close to the rocks, you might rise a nice trout.

It is a long cast and you managed all but the last much-needed yard. Rather than strain unnecessarily for that final yard, is there any way of wading it carefully? You can't move an inch further across the river, I know. Can you drop down a bit and then ease out into the main stream? Well done, that may be enough. See if you can reach now—and remember to put in some casting practice before the season is over to lengthen your maximum by several yards.

The fly is floating down excellently positioned this time—and it's been taken! Your rod tip has the bends and a fat half-pounder has dashed downstream and into deeper water. By the time you've netted him and dried the fly, the sun will be dropping behind the trees and business should start getting brisker.

One or two trout are now moving in the faster water. I suggest you come upstream about fifty yards and position yourself at the lower end of the main current's run, where it fans out and loses its pace. I think you should try a darker fly now—a Black Gnat is likely to be a closer representation of what's on the water than the Tup, which I always consider a sunshine fly.

A trout is moving exactly opposite the dock leaf over there. See him? Can you reach? Yes, your fly has gone over him once at least. Unfortunately he had risen only a moment before it arrived and you will often find such fish reluctant to upset their rising 'rhythm'. For some reason, you will come across trout which show up at almost fixed intervals, not varying their rise procedure one bit. Why this should be I don't know, since their food can hardly come downstream with similar mathematical precision. Faced with one of these bounders, try and note his 'frequency'. He may be rising once, twice or half a dozen times a minute. When you have some idea of the frequency you can time your cast accordingly, offering him the fly *just* before you anticipate his next rise.

That trout has shown twice. There he goes again! Roughly half-minute intervals between rises. I'll give you a countdown and we'll see if the system works for him. Get your fly in the air now and offer it within the next five seconds. He moved to it, very definitely, but he's a choosy one. He might think differently when it gets darker. As he is not frightened—a trout ignores a fly without any alarm as a rule—you might as well leave him for the moment. There are a couple of fish on the go now nearer midstream. Wade up five yards and you'll be able to cover both of them.

The first was too quick for you. Not a big trout, one of the fast movers which needed an instantaneous strike. The second was almost too easy. He took the fly like a little salmon, showing head, back fin and tail in a slow roll; you struck correctly as his tail started going under; only a fraction less than $\frac{3}{4}$lb.

The sun has set, only its glow remains in the sky. The river is starting to look dark and mysterious, as it always does towards dusk, and there are myriads of flies and midges (mainly midges!) swarming over the surface. You have about threequarters of an hour left to fish, and the faster water and most of the rising trout ahead of you. Put up your No 12 Pheasant Tail and grease it well. It's a nice light tying with good quality hackles and should stand up well on the water.

A quarter of an hour and not a fish? Sometimes it happens that way. But I think it will pay you to keep trying, slowly working your way up the run. The trout will suddenly start obliging. Did you see that fish splash just below you? Let the fly go on floating downstream with your next cast and he may grab it, even though you are almost on top of it. There, he has it! Extraordinary fish, trout. You could have tickled his head with the rod tip—and downstream of you. He looks between $\frac{1}{2}$lb and $\frac{3}{4}$lb.

You ought to dry your fly before casting again. See! It's refusing to float more than a foot in the faster water and probably looks a thoroughly unpalatable and waterlogged morsel. You haven't wasted any time after all. It's only the work of a moment to squeeze a fly in the amadou pad and re-grease it.

The light is going fast now, although you can still see rises and watch your fly bobbing down. Keep calm and you should pick up another brace.

You missed that fish, I suspect, because your strike wasn't firm enough. A fly like a Pheasant Tail, tied with a thick, stiffish hackle, may mask the hook point slightly in the trout's mouth. Of course, any fly fisherman expects a percentage of misses and the figure will depend on his own skill and the mood of the trout. Incidentally, your fly shouldn't be soaked after so short an immersion. Hold the cast a few inches from the end and rap the fly smartly against the dry top of your wader to shake out any moisture.

Another fish missed—you were casting too long a line and the fast water was bringing the fly down towards you too quickly. The river is narrow here and it's almost dark. Shorten your line drastically and step up the frequency of your casting. Let the fly float down a yard and no more, then lift and repeat the cast.

Got him! It was almost bound to happen in that spot. But you held him far too hard, made him thrash on the surface and positively scooped him up in the net, breaking the cast in the process. However, you caught him, that's the main thing. Only a small one but still sizeable.

You've done extremely well this evening, but you would have had several more of those midstreamers if you had struck faster. You must ask your brain to move your wrist quicker at all costs, especially when you go grayling and dace fishing!

CHAPTER FIVE

TROUT: *Brook Fishing—Sunk Fly*

I GREATLY enjoy brook fishing for trout, and many of my early days were spent on a Worcestershire brook which held a good stock of trout averaging three to the pound. From it I caught my first pounder, and subsequently one or two more such monsters. This was Leigh brook, a typical well-bushed lowland stream, winding through lush meadows and past hopyards to join the River Teme not far from Worcester.

Ideally, you should purchase a second rod if you are going in for much brook or small river trouting. Let it be 7ft or 7ft 6in at most and something like a fairy wand in weight. Providing other tackle, reel, line, etc, suits the rod, there is no reason to buy a complete outfit. Basically, the shorter rod excepted, nothing need differ when you go brook fishing. You will tie a shorter cast, of course, to suit the rod and the often limited casting space at your disposal. There is certainly no call to use finer tackle. There are places in brooks where a hooked trout has to be held hard to keep him out of trouble when, on a big river, you might allow a fish the same weight to take line.

What is so pleasant about brook fishing is the feeling it gives you of being absolutely part of your surroundings. You wade quietly into a stickle at the end of a half-mile of water, sunk between high, bushy banks, and a couple of hours later you emerge at the top end having seen no one and heard nothing but the calls of birds and the splash of rising fish. You are constantly challenged by the difficulty of inserting the fly in suitable places, and the wave in some shallow run as a three-quarter-pounder turns at the fly or nymph is a thrilling affair, often seen at very close quarters.

Moorland brooks such as Wales and Devon provide can be as difficult as any river in Britain when running low and clear, and it is a fallacy to consider brook trout small and easily caught. If you can time a visit to a moorland brook when a flood is running off, and throw a fly on it during the deadly hour or so when the black of the peat water is turning to a delicious 'sherry' gold, you will experience Lilliputian fishing at its liveliest.

In brooks, as in larger rivers, there will be times when surface fly is called for and times for the sunk fly. In general, the trout will not be too fussy about patterns. The smaller the water the bigger the fly you can tie on. Brook trout appreciate a mouthful. But whereas you could search larger rivers downstream with the sunk fly, casting a great length of line on a brook is out of the question. The banks are seldom easy to walk down, making wading essential. This rules out close-range fishing downstream. So the fly should be fished upstream, cast or catapulted into every likely place, while you creep up first one bank, then the other, and sometimes wade quietly in midstream.

You will have to become adept at stalking fish, or stalking into position to fish places where you *hope* fish will be. You will fish the water constantly, thankful when you see a trout move but never waiting for this to happen.

Some brooks are crystal clear and their trout can be watched taking or rejecting the fly. Leigh brook, by way of contrast, was typical of the rather muddy kind : inclined to be dour and lacking in good rises—though not fish. On that type of water the cast tells you when a trout has taken the fly, or there is an underwater movement prompting response.

Brook trout have a habit of lying beneath undercut banks and in the deep holes left by floods. They fancy tree roots or the trunks of fallen trees as places of safety, and they tuck themselves tightly under alder and willow trees whose branches trail in the water. Other good holding places are around boulders or between weed beds where there is some current and a depth of a foot or more.

The technique of casting a fly to these fish will not be learned in a day—which is why we started off on the less exacting fishing of the small river. Finesse is all-important on brooks. The technique of casting the sunk fly upstream has been described already. If it sinks slowly and takes not more than six inches of the cast under with it, that is ample. The fly at this depth can be seen by the trout, whose take should equally well be seen by the angler. If no underwater movement is spotted the sudden draw of the remainder of the cast is always unmistakable.

It is surprising how *little* room is needed to cast a fly satisfactorily. There are places on overgrown brooks where the rod literally cannot be held upright and you have to stoop under branches as you wade upstream. Yet from such streams the bag may average as high in numbers and weight as a bag from a well-known big river.

PRACTICE

This clear and tiny stream is the Dulas, a tributary of the Irfon which is itself a Wye tributary. The Irfon is quite like the upper Wye, a full-blooded, rocky river difficult to wade and containing plenty of chub and dace in addition to its trout. The Dulas, on the other hand, is a moorland brook flowing only a few miles before reaching its parent river. And in the stretch I've chosen for this July day there are no dace or salmon parr—just trout. The fish here are plentiful and active, but not easily taken on a bright warm day like this. You should have some fun offering them an upstream nymph.

Other, perhaps wiser anglers are sunbathing up on the hills until evening. It may be hard work, but I'm going to try and prove that you can catch a bag of middling trout even on dog days like this without having to rely on the evening rise.

I like your 7ft split cane rod. It's a delightfully switchy little weapon, very light to handle, a real wrist-action caster. You were sensible enough to buy a second reel, I see, also small and light. It pays to have a spare in case something goes amiss. Does it fit your 9ft rod, and does your first reel fit the 7ft rod? Good, that's sensible.

My cast for this style of fishing is not more than six feet long, tapering from 5lb down to an 18in length of 2lb nylon. Fly pattern matters no more than the pattern of your shirt. Tie on a

High banks can make casting tricky, but fish love them, especially when trees grow along them too!

Concealment is important when fly fishing. Wading is one way . . .

and crawling is another and probably better way

Pheasant Tail nymph size 15. The line and the first yard or four feet of your cast will float: the fine point (as the final link is known) must sink through the surface film.

You've seen for yourself, walking through the meadows, some lengths of the Dulas are open and parts of it flow through tunnels of trees. There are some lovely flats and glides, and some attractive fast water gushing over and through rocks: all this, of course, on a very miniature scale.

Here we are at your starting point. Sit down and study the situation. Immediately in front of you there is a strong run of current under your own bank. There are no obstacles to casting save a few tufts of marshy grass and a hedge some yards downstream. Above this run is a pool, perhaps fifteen yards long, with one or two scattered boulders at the top end. There are certainly trout at the tail and head of this pool. It is gin clear and shallow and will tax your ingenuity. Above the pool there are several 'steps down' where the stream has created minor waterfalls over the years. The rocks are dark and mossy, and the water boils over them in a mass of white foam and bubbles. There, too, trout will be lying, but the nymph will have to be fished 'blind' while you creep up from the pool below.

And now, while you are soaking that nymph and cast, take a look at the present I've brought you. It's known as a hook hone, and in future I want you to make very good use of it. Hook points often become slightly turned or blunted and you will learn soon enough that some flies fresh from their makers are tied on undeniably blunt or coarse hooks. A truly *sharp* hook is all-important when fishing. I'm constantly checking mine against my fingers.

It's going to be creeping and crawling from now on, so let's see what you can do with the fly on a hot summer afternoon. Minnow and worm are not allowed here!

Don't get too close to the water. A rod's length away is about right. The current is under your bank. Use a gentle overhead cast and drop the fly just beyond the grass fringe on our bank, lifting the rod point and drawing it downstream almost immediately. When you have wriggled another yard or two away from the hedge you can work your rod point parallel with the bank and throw the fly upstream.

Your vigorous and totally unnecessary false casting must have dried out the nymph and the cast. Keep the nymph soaked!

That troutlet took the fly on the surface, I'm certain. He is undersized even for the Dulas, so hold the point and let him wriggle off downstream of you.

Why ignore the best bit of water? I mean that square yard or so where the main stream from the pool above drops over its gravel sill and starts the run you have been fishing. Drop your nymph right into that minor turmoil of water, cast it gently into the draw of the current above if need be, making it appear a natural tit-bit to the trout which is certainly waiting there. A good tug, that! He was on and off in a flash. These trout are really quick.

That trout in midstream a yard up from the tail of the pool is going to be the most difficult fish you've tackled yet. You daren't get too close to him, but if you cast from below the pull of the current will seize your line and make a mockery of the nymph's action. Also, unless you keep your head and rod tip down, the fish will see too much and become suspicious. He will undoubtedly be suspicious when the cast falls near him.

Those are your difficulties. On the credit side you have not alarmed him yet, and a certain amount of drag is not only permissible but actually desirable with the nymph. Can you creep on your stomach until you are opposite the trout, but stay well back in the meadow? And can you then side-cast making the nymph drop a couple of feet above him and well to your side of him? If you can manage this *gently* and first time I think he will grab your fly. It all depends on your skill.

Well done! You hooked him instantly and he's so annoyed he's jumped all over the pool, scaring the daylights out of his quarter-pound pals in the lower half. He weighs an ounce more than they do, so keep him if you wish, but before handing him up to me, wipe your nymph and the last foot of cast in his slime and gill blood. I don't know whether the scent of blood lingers on the nymph but it certainly helps sink it quickly and it's a harmless practice—with dead fish—that could possibly be to your advantage.

The head of this pool is the only other place in it worth trying after all that disturbance. The stream spills out from the rock steps above, not in one concentrated gush but on a wide front. You have three or four yards of possible holding water so it will pay you to cover it with a cast into every six inches of the stream's width. Drop the fly right in the tiny waterfall the last rock step creates, and don't be satisfied until you have done so.

Another lively little trout, almost at the last possible cast across to the far bank. Unlike the others which must have been feeding there, he saw nothing of the cast attached to your fly. He is an honest quarter-pounder.

Now for the rock steps. Four of them, topped by a deeper swirly hole. The difficulty here is, of course, lack of elbow room. That handsome old oak tree has put out a branch which leans over the stream in a decidedly anti-piscatorial manner, and the fishable water in each step isn't much more than a yard square.

Make yourself part of the landscape here, though it takes the skin from your kneecaps! Make frequent short casts, keeping the rod tip on a level with the water and 'wristing' the fly into position.

Nothing but a hunk of moss from the first step. A swirl on the surface in the second, but he wouldn't come again. A miniature trout from the third, hardly an ounce I guess, which you pulled clean from the water when starting another cast, to your mutual astonishment. He was well hooked, too, and a good example of the trout that takes unseen no matter how carefully you watch for the rise or movement. He swam off in lively style after you unhooked him. From the fourth step, nothing.

Don't move up any more. Try a cast into the swirly pool above. Ah! You saw that one draw the cast under, and struck him very capably. Such little pools always hold good fish. When he is beaten you can draw him down the 'waterfall' and net him at your feet. A good fish—6oz.

You are probably astonished at the time it has taken to fish this stretch of water and catch these trout. You started over an hour and a half ago and you are not yet 100 yards from the hedge. Had the day been duller and the brook coloured by rain, you could have walked and waded up thrice as fast, catching trout with ease. In these hot conditions you were forced to go slow, and it paid off handsomely.

Let's walk upstream, skirting the next hundred yards which is rather a millrace and a brambly, bushy one at that, to try the next long flat. If you wade quietly up the right bank you will be reasonably well concealed. There is a good spot half way up this flat where a tree bole thrusts itself out into the brook creating a larder for the trout. There are usually three or four fish bulging around it—by bulging I mean taking nymphs underwater and making a rise form without showing themselves.

You will be faced here with yet another of the numerous little problems besetting fly fishermen: how to drop the nymph close enough to the downstream trout without disturbing him or his immediate neighbour only a foot upstream. If it drops on his nose he may be scared. If it drops on his upstream neighbour's tail both may be scared. Try fishing it short of them in the hope that one of them will spot it and come charging out to take.

No, these trout are too well placed. The set of the current, slight though it is, means that everything they feed on goes under and around the tree bole and close to it. They are not accustomed to moving off their lucrative beat. Try casting the nymph softly against the tree itself and allowing it to drop into the water. There, a trout had it and was off double quick.

That seems to have stopped all the fun. Hang on for a few minutes and something may move again. There now! A small trout moved downstream of you at the hinge of the pool, that last deadly bit of smooth-flowing water just before it breaks up in a rapid. Don't worry about your position: try a downstream cast back-handed and give the nymph a series of gentle jerks playing it across his nose.

He made a real rise form in the water as he took it and you responded quickly. This one is of debatable size. Why not give him the benefit of the doubt?

Strange, nothing has risen by the tree again. Try a cast on the off-chance. It may be that the supply of natural food has temporarily dried up.

What happened then? I saw you strike and positively heard the 'ping' as your cast snapped. The line must have got trapped somehow, probably around the reel handle. The trout dived for home, your rod tip sprang down and on an almost direct pull the fish simply broke the fly off without difficulty. Never mind. The sun is still shining, there are plenty more fish between us and the top boundary and *your* trout will come to no harm from the Pheasant Tail nymph. He will be able to rub it out very quickly.

Just look at that lovely bit of water where the brook swirls through rounded boulders over golden gravel. If there is a fisherman's heaven, it surely holds just such a stretch of water with the same quarter-pounders incessantly on the move.

CHAPTER SIX

TROUT: *Brook Fishing—Surface Fly*

THEORY

THERE'S little I need say about the theory of fishing surface fly upstream in brooks. It follows exactly the same pattern as fishing the same fly in larger waters, or indeed fishing the nymph upstream.

I have on occasions used two surface flies on a cast. This method covers more water with each cast made but has the disadvantage of creating drag for both flies. The dropper is tied on in just the same way as a sunk fly, but with a shorter length of nylon from the cast knot.

Another method of fishing surface fly in brooks, and larger waters too, is to dap it. This is a very old dodge and it is highly probable that fishing with the surface fly began in this way. You will need a longer rod than the 7ft caster for dapping. Let it be your nine-footer or, preferably, a coarse fishing rod of about 12ft. The tackle consists of a yard of reasonably stout nylon cast attached to the reel line, and a weight of some sort attached to the cast a foot or 18in above the fly.

Dapping is an invaluable method of dropping a fly over a rising fish which could not possibly be reached with a normal cast. You creep along the bank, keeping well back from the edge of the brook, and wheedle the rod tip, weight and fly through the tree branches, bushes or other obstructions, which make the chosen place so inaccessible. The weight, by the way, is simply a large split shot or a very small drilled lead held in place by a shot pinched on the nylon. It should be reeled right up to the rod point and held there until that point is in its correct position—over the fish.

Line should be gently unreeled until the fly touches the surface.

Sometimes a trout will have it instantly; if not, they may come after the fly has been 'dapped' up and down a few times, making little rings on the surface like a bluebottle in distress. This is a deadly method of fly fishing providing your approach is cautious, and providing you lower the fly carefully and allow none of the cast to lie on the surface.

It is essentially a method in which movement of the fly pays. You are imitating some unfortunate mite which has dropped from a tree or the high bank and is struggling for its life. The excitement of the method is obvious. You are virtually on top of the trout and may well see it rise. Don't be tempted to strike as it comes up but allow it to mouth the fly and be turning down with it before lifting sharply in response. How you retrieve a played-out trout all adds to the fun!

Again, pattern of fly doesn't much matter. The trout is attracted by the natural movement. Sometimes they will actually rush up and take your fly while it is on the dangle *above* the water.

If the artificial fly fails you, the natural should not. Bluebottles and house flies, crane flies (Daddy Longlegs), grasshoppers and even woodlice can usefully be pressed into service for dapping. The more 'buzz' or 'kick' they possess the better they will attract fish. There is at least one useful pattern of dapping hook on the market which has a small spring-clip attachment making it easier to hold the naturals; but an ordinary hook through their middles serves almost as well.

Dapping is one of the few methods of fishing a fly which succeeds on hot summer afternoons when trout are indifferent if not positively sleepy. There are invariably a few fish looking upwards for unexpected tit-bits along heavily grown stretches of river bank.

PRACTICE

Leigh brook is one of the few trout fisheries in a county where coarse fish predominate. The stretch we are visiting is divided by a weir. Above it there is a long stretch of 'dead' water where trout seldom rise—a float fisherman's stretch. Below the weir, the brook becomes a lively trout stream again with a series of pools connected by fast flowing runs. It winds like a snake's tail through the undergrowth, in places cutting deeply into the red Worcestershire soil. Unfortunately the water isn't very clear. You cannot see the bottom where it is more than 18in deep.

We are going to make a day of it, and at some stage we hope to see mayfly hatching and being taken greedily by the trout. In this, and most other parts of Britain, mayfly hatch in the first fortnight of June. They are the largest water flies of interest to anglers and where they hatch in quantity their short season does induce the trout—including some big trout which normally take nothing else on top—to rise with abandon at times.

We won't go into the history of the mayfly, except to mention that it follows much the same pattern as other river flies but takes longer to develop from egg to finished article. It is an easy fly to imitate—I mean imitate in this case—and is absolutely unmistakable on the water owing to its size. Leigh brook has plenty of mud along its bed which suits the mayfly larva. They hatch into green or grey duns twice the size of other flies.

You are going to fish upstream, as you did on the Dulas, starting at the bottom boundary and keeping a watchful eye for any signs of mayfly. Hatches of fly vary from day to day, and so do the times of their emergence. You ought to see a few before midday, though I think here the best chance may come later.

Why not try my twin surface fly idea? Tie your dropper not more than 18in from the tail fly. They could be as close as a foot. In such cramped surroundings they must be close. Many of the runs where trout feed here are only a couple of feet wide and they will not move out of them for a small dry fly.

Casting isn't quite so easy with two up. It feels just a little woolly, but two flies drop almost as sweetly as one on the water. Wade in, and if you stick to midstream the light 7ft rod will have ample room to manœuvre. There is an extremely high bank on our side, good for dapping, and a steady flow of current beneath it with two or three resident trout.

Don't worry about the effect of the mayfly hatches on other fly and feeding fish. Trout will normally take the usual small fly before the mayfly shows up and may even take them in preference to the mayfly at times. You may easily pick up a trout or two on your Tup and Greenwell. Start casting up that likely run and see what happens. It's a quarter past ten and going to be a scorcher of a day.

Well, you had the satisfaction of seeing one small trout swirl up at the dropper. There's no need to linger once you have fished the run—there are many equally good places to try further upstream.

The next holding spot is the swift tail of the pool above, complicated by a strand of barbed wire across the brook to prevent cattle 'poaching'. The wire is a couple of feet above the water so you can switch the flies at least as far beneath and beyond it, and that should be enough.

A quiet rise to the tail fly and away goes the trout upstream for a few yards. Turn him, otherwise he will spoil things at the top of the pool. He can be beached here in the cattle drink, a fish of nearly $\frac{1}{2}$lb. He looks fat, I suspect his fly diet in the past week or two has been rich.

Still no sign of the mayfly. Here is some faster water running deep and attractive on both sides of an 'island' that obviously used to be the mainland. There are fish both sides, but the left bank is easier, and better holding water. Try it first.

Marvel of marvels, two rises and you have hooked one of the trout on your dropper. That can't happen very often in this brook where the trout are by no means numerous compared with a stream like the Dulas. Take care of your tail fly when you net him. A tiddler! Back he must go.

The next stretch of water is a swirling glide that will tax your casting abilities. The brook flows round a right-hand bend, looking downstream towards you, and there are partially sunk tree branches on your left and a whole tree trunk in the brook on your right as you wade up. You may not like the situation, but the trout do!

Wait—there's a mayfly floating down like a miniature sailing boat. Will it reach you? Gone! So you know there's one trout on the alert alongside the tree trunk. Yes . . . one or two more mayflies coming. It's time to take off that cast and substitute the slightly stronger one we prepared tapering to 4lb b.s. This isn't because we anticipate bigger trout. A fly like a mayfly on a large hook demands a rather heavier cast. It's a question of the correct balance of tackle combined with the need for extra firm striking. Larger hooks need a firmer pull home.

That trout by the tree trunk has taken every mayfly floating downstream so far. He ought to be easy meat for your artificial. You have some attractive models in the tin, cork bodies and wings exactly the size and colour of the natural Green Drake, as this variety of mayfly is known. Put one up, by all means, though I fear its beauty may be spoiled by the trout whose teeth are sharp enough to tear delicate materials. I have some buzzy, hackled models which kill just as well and prove less troublesome to dry and spruce up after killing a fish. You're welcome to try them later.

I expect you've noticed the tree trunk fish has been joined by another, rising downstream but scarcely a yard away and picking up the stragglers among the mayfly. You had better cast to that one first. Remember, the fly is a sizeable morsel with those two large wings attached to it so do *not* strike too quickly.

Offer him your artificial between his rises at the natural. Don't place it on the water alongside a real mayfly or it will merely demonstrate the superiority of the natural article. Fortunately there isn't too much natural about. The trout are keen for more, and that is the ideal state of affairs.

Place your fly well upstream of the rising trout. He is nearer midstream than his neighbour, who shouldn't be disturbed by a quiet cast. Your cast and line ought to drift down here without any drag on the fly since you are wading in the main current and throwing nearly directly upstream.

The trout met your fly beautifully. Your strike was well timed, but as you failed to hook him I can only imagine you were not firm enough and the coarser hook point and barb failed to pull in. He won't show up again for a while, but our first friend by the tree trunk is still hard at it. If you hook him he will certainly try a dive under that trunk—you have been warned!

Hooked! And what a tugging match! He was really determined to go home, and you and the little rod were very nearly beaten. It was as well you held on, because to have allowed him another foot of line would have meant losing both fish and fly. There's still plenty of life in him, so take care! After those good runs up and down the pool he is tugging again, putting his head down with real determination and banging the cast every so often with his tail.

Have the net open and well sunk by your feet. Your trout ought to be virtually played out when you finally lift him to the surface after that battle. Here he comes, swirling forlornly with never a jump. Ease him towards you, lift the net and when he's safely in it drop the handle slightly towards the water again, trapping him in the meshes and making it impossible for him to jump or struggle out.

That's a grand, sturdy fish and your best yet. He's 14oz and a very good trout for the brook. Now retrieve the wreck of your fly and prepare for more fun. The mayfly hatch won't necessarily last long.

The spot you've reached now is a deep, swirly hole and the taking trout will be lying where the current leaves it in about two feet of water. Make sure you throw a slack line here or the fly may drag badly. Drop it somewhere near the centre of the pool and let the current bring it down naturally on the correct line.

You've risen him! This one is a surface fighter, don't hold too hard he's well out in midstream. Ah . . . the fly has come away and shot up into the branches above. You were altogether too tough on that trout. You should fight it out with them like that only if to give them line means losing them for certain. You could have allowed that trout a couple of yards run in any direction.

Here's a very slow-moving stretch of water, but there's often a trout on the prowl so watch the mayfly closely.

One gone, two gone. The same trout I believe, cruising round instead of waiting for his meals to come to him. These fish can be awkward because you never know quite where they'll be next. You may well cast too far and frighten them with the line, or put the fly on their tails.

On this placid water the fly will sit almost motionless. You must leave it alone and be patient, the trout may suddenly become aware of it and glide up to take it. My plan would be to try half a dozen casts and if I hadn't caught the trout's eye by then I should reckon him a frightened fish. This is, of course, entirely dependent on the trout's continued rising.

Third time lucky. He came to you very confidently, but he was a slow riser and your strike was so prompt you only nicked his nose.

Round the corner, part of the charm of such brook fishing, is an entirely different piece of fishing. A fast, deep length of water, it can only be waded half way up which enables you to cover it all. You then have to wade downstream again to get out up the bank. The mayfly hatch seems to be over : just a straggler or two here and there. Try this run with your Green Drake and then it will be time for a very late lunch.

No response. That's a good indication—especially from this particular run—that the rise is over. It is very warm and as you want to stay on for the evening rise I suggest a sleep after lunch and then a quiet hour or so of dapping.

I have brought one of my coarse rods for dapping. It's 11ft long and made of hollow fibre glass. I'll set up the tackle in just the way I mentioned earlier. The fly may as well be a size 12 Palmer, a nice fat, bushy object tied with plenty of stiff, brown hackles. Notice, the hackle is tied all down the body of the fly and not just at the eye. It is an excellent floater and meant to represent a multitude of the natural, 'buzzy' objects which descend on rivers whirring their wings.

Now we are refreshed enough to stroll the fifty yards upstream to the weir pool with our dapping rod. Actually the weir pool can be fished in a normal way too, but there is a high wall above the left bank with several hawthorn bushes sprouting from it making it a very suitable place for the dap. One of the main runs of current from the weir will be right under your rod tip, which will only protrude a few inches over the top of the wall. You will find it easy enough to squeeze between the bushes.

Very slowly, ease the rod top, the lead and fly over the water. The cast is reeled right up, of course, the lead actually held against the top rod ring. When you are positioned correctly begin unreeling line so that the fly drops towards the water. Peep carefully over the bank in order to control its descent and ensure it reaches the water but drops no further.

When it touches the surface raise and lower the rod tip fractionally so that your fly sets up the slight disturbance that might be expected of a natural. Let it drift down current as far as your limited rod movement will allow, then lift and repeat the process.

When you've dapped unsuccessfully for a minute or two it's time to wind up and try the next place. Trout usually respond quickly or not at all to the dap, although some anglers reckon you can tease them into taking by making your fly jump up and down on the water incessantly. Trout like to command their own little pockets of water so I never hesitate to dap at yard intervals, assuming one can reach the water at such regular intervals. Try round the next bush, and then the next.

The rod tip shows there was an eager trout towards the tail of the pool, and he hooked himself since the rise obviously took you aback. Playing a fish from above enables you to exert deadly control over him. This one was beaten and swimming in tired circles in less than half a minute.

Extracting hooked trout from the water is half the fun of dapping. I suggest you get right down on your stomach and lean as far over the water as possible with the net in your left hand. Grasp the rod by its middle joint and draw it back towards you, swinging the trout closer to the bank. There's not much scope for finesse netting this half-pounder. If you can reach him, scoop him up and then wriggle your way backwards, allowing the reel to give line freely or you may strain the top of the rod or break the cast.

The sun is dropping now and it's a lovely warm evening. There seem to be some swarms of fly above the weir and up towards the bridge, so let's walk up and investigate. As I thought, the 'spent gnat', as dying mayfly are called, are on the water in their scores and hundreds. It is obviously going to be a very big 'fall'. There are two or three very good fish rising close to the bridge where you never normally see anything take a fly. They are cruising round taking their fill of the dying flies which seem to be massed on the surface. You will indeed be fortunate to get a rise in these circumstances.

You have a spent mayfly pattern in your box, its wings splayed out to lie in the water like the natural. Drop it close to the spot where each of those trout put their noses up most often. There is precious little flow here, so be careful how you lift to make a fresh cast or you will frighten the fish.

As I feared, there is so much fly the trout will not look at your artificial. Mayfly in their myriads are dropping on the surface of the brook and any rising trout will soon be surfeited. It is an extraordinary sight to see so many large flies all over the brook, their brief day or two's existence in the air almost at an end. Their whole existence leads up to a tremendous climax and a sudden drop back to the element which gave them birth. Even the birds have tired of swooping among so many flies. We had better try some of the pools below the weir. There may not be quite so much fly down there.

I call this the Big Pool, and it's my favourite on the brook. The current follows a gentle curve under the far bank and the trout I expected to find is rising under the small alder half way round the curve.

Into him! And I'll tell you why. Your line was trapped in the slack water in the centre of the pool and caused the fly to drag under and across his nose at just the right moment. He couldn't stop himself grabbing the unlikely object. We don't always catch trout in the way we intend. This one is five or six ounces and really bulging with mayfly: look at them all around his mouth.

Three more likely pools drawn blank, and masses of spent mayfly about, even plastered over your waders. It's getting towards the end of the day and I think we might make the next pool the last. I've kept an eye on the fast run-in at the top but seen no sign of a fish; nor has anything moved lower down.

Try a few casts in the fast water. No good? Well, as a last resort, give your fly a soaking and pull it across that run underwater. See that golden flash as a trout turned? You might have caught him with a mayfly nymph pattern, but somehow I doubt it. Never mind, it's been a grand day.

CHAPTER SEVEN

TROUT: *Lowland Reservoir—Sunk Fly Fishing*

THEORY

RESERVOIR trouting is very different from river fishing. The fish is the same but its habits are very different. Most lowland reservoirs contain rich feeding for their fish. Consequently you may scarcely see a rising trout for days if conditions aren't just right. And the fishing so often turns out to be a minor variation of salmon fishing—long hours of casting and waiting for the pull that may or may not come. On the credit side, you may get a very large trout indeed from some of the famous reservoirs. What's more, salmon-like, you may get it within a minute of wading in to start fishing.

The main difference between river and reservoir trout is that the latter *must* roam for their food. Often they are several feet down, bottom-grubbing, and these are the occasions when flies must be deeply sunk. If the trout are showing on the surface the game becomes more interesting, though not always more rewarding.

Some reservoirs are very large indeed with miles of bank from which to fish, and a collection of boats, too. Boating we will deal with in the next section. Personally I prefer bank fishing and consider it the deadlier method of taking trout on the sunk fly.

With the exception of the 'concrete bowl' type of reservoir, most of the man-made waters in this country take advantage of natural contours and the only sign that you are on a reservoir will be the dam. There will be shallows at the top end and generally a large, deep area of water towards the dam, which shelves up into a shallow again. There will be bays and underwater contours to learn; large areas of muddy bottom and some precious places where gravel or shingle crop up. Most reservoirs become very weedy along their shallows in the summer.

When trout are feeding there are normally enough to interest you along the margins. Plenty of fish will be seen out over the deeps, particularly when a good breeze is blowing from bank to bank, but it's surprising how many good drifts in a boat fail to produce a trout until the marginal shallows are reached. This is because trout generally browse along the margins in up to six feet of water. If they are feeding deeper than this they will prove difficult to catch. When there is a breeze—and reservoir fishermen pray for that desirable state of affairs from the first day of the season to the last—the trout often head into it, feeding on whatever it chances to bring towards them.

On a river, I should advocate plenty of movement on the part of the fisherman, casting for virtually stationary fish. On a reservoir, the trout fisherman will lose nothing by emulating the heron, standing still, casting continuously and allowing the fish to come to him. True, there are times when it pays to search the water, wading quietly along and covering a number of likely places on reservoirs, but I can say quite truthfully I have always done best with the sunk lure fished on 'standstill' principles.

Reservoirs seldom present casting problems, save the achievement of phenomenal distances from the banks which are not often needed. Let's face it: if you can cast twenty yards you are sure to see trout rising twenty-five yards off which set your heart aching with desire to drop a fly on their noses. When you have achieved the extra five yards you will realise with not a little frustration there are *still* trout moving five yards out of reach. As a beginner, if you can manage a fifteen-yard cast you will be doing very well indeed and missing very little.

Conditions on any reservoir will vary from absolute calm to a rough 'sea' whipped up by gale-force winds. Trout are invariably easier to catch in a good wave caused by a steady breeze. It seems to set them moving on the surface and by casting across their feeding lines you may have good results. These lines are often discernible by the white scum on the water surface.

The easiest breezes to tackle are the ones coming from your right or left, for they carry the fly or flies better than a breeze

Reservoirs can be attractive places. This is Kennick, one of the South West Devon Water Board's reservoirs on the fringe of Dartmoor

Rainbow trout spawning. These fish have found very few British rivers to their liking

directly facing or behind you and certainly help you fish them better. More about this in the practical section. Dead calms require caution—obviously. Trout cannot be expected to tolerate heavy lines landing with a splash in their vicinity. Some anglers insist on surface fly in a calm. Without being dogmatic, my choice would be a sunk line and lure which creates less disturbance when the fly is retrieved.

Many lowland reservoirs are stocked with brown and rainbow trout. Rainbows are the closest thing to sea trout you can find in enclosed British waters. They are silvery fish with a handsome pink sheen down their sides, they grow quickly, take lures savagely and fight with tremendous dash, much faster than brownies. They are great fun.

Don't be alarmed about tackle requirements. If your financial position is 'average', use the 9ft rod and reel, line and casts already recommended. Indeed, river flies will take reservoir trout perfectly well, though I think you would be wise to equip yourself with a few reservoir specialities.

I would take the light 9ft outfit into a boat very happily, but for lure fishing from the bank I advise a slightly heavier rod capable of standing plenty of casting against the breeze with a heavy line. Single-handed casting becomes tough work with a rod of over 10ft; select one of 9ft 6in to 10ft for the strong-arm stuff and you can use it happily for sea trout and salmon fishing too. With this rod you will require an HDH line which will make the rod work and so achieve the lengthier casts sometimes desirable on reservoirs.

Strictly speaking, you ought to have two lines of similar weight, one a floater and the other a sinker to fish lures deep and steadily. My first choice is the floater, but the sinker is another dual-purpose item for it can be used for spring salmon fishing in small rivers. To both these lines I blood knot a yard of 10lb nylon which forms the top of the cast, dispensing with a line-to-cast knot. Normally this lasts for a season. The illustration overleaf shows how to do it.

I have read some stories of wild runs by large reservoir trout, and much advice about the need to have 100 yards of backing attached to one's thirty yards or so of casting line. How a fish of under 3lb can put up to 100 yards distance between itself and

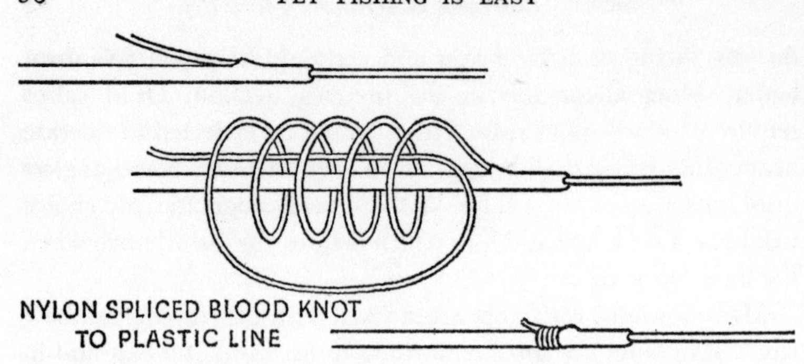

the angler I've not yet discovered! Twice only has my backing appeared when playing reservoir brownies, and both were foul-hooked fish of less than 2lb. Generally the take is the only moment when a reservoir trout endangers tackle, and if it is properly cushioned by the bend of your rod, perhaps coupled with a curved or slack line, the rest ought to be easy.

Playing large trout, and sea trout and salmon, becomes much less frightening when you realise they only run hard and fast when subjected to great pressure. If you *will* stand there clenching your teeth and holding so hard that the rod tip is almost hooped into the water you must expect the fish to stick its head down and keep on going. Ease the pressure off entirely or change the angle of the rod and the fish will oblige by altering course or stopping. The further a fish moves away from you, the more you must ease rod pressure, otherwise the weight of the drowned line in the water may tear the fly from his mouth or even cause a break.

Most of my reservoir trout have been taken on $2\frac{1}{2}$lb to 5lb b.s. casts. Beginners should select the heavier one and gradually go finer as they gain experience of the fish. One or two water companies recommend heavier casts still, and beginners should certainly follow their advice.

. . . which brings us to the fly. I would not be without some Butchers, Worm flies, and some simple black-hackled creations with peacock herl bodies rejoicing in various names which are taken for nymphs or snails. I also like Peter Ross, Mallard and Claret and the Zulu. Black is a very good trout fly colour, hence the perennial appeal of the Black and Peacock Spider and Zulu.

I like some of the small flies to be tied on double hooks which,

I think, gain a better purchase in the large jaws of the bigger trout, besides sinking quicker. Some lures should be large, up to size 6, which is a salmon size, but many reservoir trout fall victims every season to sizes 15 and 16 as used on rivers. The rougher the day, the larger the fly you should put up and the faster you can fish it.

How many flies you attach to your cast depends on you. If you are fishing the sunk lure, imitating a small fish and inviting trout deep down to chase it, one fly is all you should attach to the cast. Ideally it should be fished with a sinking line. When the line goes down almost to the level of the fly in five or six feet of water it fishes it on an even keel for a greater distance than any floating line could achieve. It looks more natural to the predatory trout.

If you are going to persuade trout that your flies are nymphs, you can tie on one or two droppers and employ your floating line. Nymphs, snails and other water creatures, commonly swim, glide or float upwards either smoothly or in short jerky movements, and this effect is easily obtained with several flies below a floating line.

Retrieving the fly is important. It should not be hauled through the water like a speedboat, but with that exception almost every method of fishing it back to the shore will catch trout. You may go in for a steady pull which moves the fly slowly all the time, or a series of greater or lesser jerks imparting life to it. You may go in for the 'sink and draw' style, allowing the flies to settle between every pull; or you may let a favourable wind put a slight belly in the line and fish the flies across the line of the oncoming trout with scarcely a movement of your hand on the line needed at all.

Remember, trout are always attracted by moving objects and just as easily frightened if the line and cast are too obtrusive. A downright lousy cast which flops across the waves of a windswept reservoir has a less obviously bad effect than the same cast on a river: but the effect *is* the same—frightened trout if any are in the vicinity.

The take of reservoir fish varies from a suspicion that something is interfering with your fly to an unmistakable thump which can pull the rod down and your arm too. The thumps come from trout which have moved some distance upwards or across to take the fly with determination and return to their previous course. They ought to be well-hooked fish if you raise the rod without haste, keeping a good bend in it.

Only experience will enable you to hit all the trout that come to your fly, and even then some will be lost. A movement under water or the sight of a trout rolling over the fly, showing his back fin, may be your clue; it may be the slightest twitch or the sight of line or cast drawing away, or a golden side glimpsed as a trout turns with your fly. At all times be ready for the large, fast trout (especially rainbow) you may meet. Do not point the rod tip along the line but angle it, a right angle if possible which 'cushions' the take, and never allow loose line to tangle over your boots, around cuff buttons or your net handle.

You are more exposed to the weather on a reservoir, so dress accordingly. Above all, don't spend your time wishing you could be fishing the middle or the far bank, and don't keep changing position or rushing from place to place. Choose what you think will prove a good place and give it a real working-over. Reservoir trout have their taking times and you may have to be patient and wait for them to sound the dinner gong.

Now let's be off to a small West Country reservoir, where day tickets are available, in the month of September.

PRACTICE

This is Durleigh reservoir near Bridgwater in Somerset. We shall fish it just as we might fish a dozen similar public waters in the West Country—first buying our cheap-at-the-price day tickets. There are brown and rainbow trout to be had here and prospects look very favourable—a light mist is already being dispersed by the sun and, more important, there's a gentle ripple across the surface of the water.

Between us we have two outfits. There is your 9ft rod with a floating line which will do to fish a team of three nymphs, and I have brought along a stouter rod of 10ft which will serve for lure fishing in conjunction with a sunk line.

Put up the 9ft rod while I deal with its big brother. Your cast goes the full length of the rod which is a good thing. If trout are being ultra-cautious I very often use a cast a yard longer. The flies should be spaced about 2ft 6in apart, all on the lower half of the cast well away from the line. Tie on a Butcher at the tail end, a Peter Ross in the middle and top it with a small Zulu as bob fly. This is a 'fancy' cast, the flies are not specifically representating either fish or natural fly life : it just so happens they are proven killers on any water !

The heavier outfit I've set up has only one fly on the 9ft cast tapering to 5lb b.s. and that's an Alexandra size 8. No need to be modest when fishing for these gluttons upwards of a pound. Did you notice, by the way, when fitting the rod sections together I gave the male ferrules a twist round in my hair? This imparts just enough grease to ensure they will not stick together whatever the weather. Believe me, a day in the rain can gum up rod ferrules badly.

The breeze is slightly in our faces, coming off the lower end of the reservoir, which is, roughly speaking, egg-shaped and cut straight at one end by the dam. You would not find it difficult to cast into the breeze now, but in half an hour it may be fresher so let's walk across the dam. There is a pleasant gravel bay over there which may hold some feeding trout.

Here you are. Before wading in, soak your cast and flies and cover the shallows. You are the first across here today and there might be an undisturbed trout feeding close in. No good? In you go, then, wading steadily until you are over knee level. This spot is close enough to the dam to be useful—trout always enjoy patrolling its stonework on the look-out for snails or fry—but far enough from it to cover the water where the breeze first catches it. Trout know they will find fly where the ripple starts.

Please yourself how you cast. You may like to drop your flies in gradually increasing arcs around you to avoid boredom. Personally I set myself a comfortable distance and go on casting to a given spot until a trout obliges.

You are fishing much too fast and not bringing the flies far enough back towards you. Think how a nymph or a tiny fish would behave in the water. They would make sudden, but slight movements. Certainly they would not proceed in swift moves a yard at a time. Retrieve your line slowly, an inch or two at a time, merely keeping in touch between pulls by drawing the line fractionally inwards.

Did you see that trout rise? He made a slight swirl in the ripple about ten yards beyond your casting limit. There he was again, showing a back fin. Where there's one on a reservoir there may well be more, so keep on searching. Try and draw your flies slowly upwards towards the end of your retrieve as they reach the shallows. Trout may follow them some distance before deciding to take. I think you could safely count ten before starting to retrieve a cast to allow the flies to sink reasonably deep.

Ah! You interested something. Felt a hasty pluck, I expect, struck belatedly and touched nothing. Possibly the fish mouthed one of your flies and got rid of it hastily, perhaps it was only playing. I've foul-hooked a lot of reservoir trout in their pectoral fins or stomachs, which suggests they must often turn over a fly playfully to drown it. Trout which pluck lightly in that way may come again providing you haven't startled them with a full-blooded strike. The secret is to keep retrieving steadily and hope for a decisive pull.

I haven't seen many rises in the last quarter of an hour, only isolated splashes probably caused by tiddlers. It looks as though you started fishing at the tag end of an early morning rise. It's now eleven o'clock and the water looks dead. I expect they'll come up again at lunchtime, or during the afternoon. Meanwhile, what about trying the other rod and the lure? It relieves the monotony to try an entirely fresh method of fly fishing after you have given one method a thorough trial.

Lure fishing is the method most likely to succeed on the cold, desolate days of spring. It is also successful when every effort with the nymph has failed, and between rises. Naturally it accounts for plenty of trout which are on the rise, but then I consider it more fun to fish a fly as if it *was* a fly.

Pick up that hefty rod and move, cautiously, on to the stonework of the dam. It's allowed here although most water undertakings do not permit fishing on or near their dams. Remember you are now using a rod with a slower but stouter action, so relax and don't hasten your movements. The line should be heavy enough to gain you five yards or so on the fifteen you were casting the nymphs. Have two spare yards in your hand to shoot as your cast goes forward.

The further the lure goes out the better. You will be retrieving it slowly, first having allowed the line and cast to sink deep. Do not retrieve every cast at equal speed. It will keep you amused if, for instance, you double or even treble the speed of your lure every sixth cast. This occasionally induces a half-asleep trout to accelerate and grab the lure.

The breeze is coming diagonally from behind your right shoulder and will give your casts plenty of lift. Incidentally, never underestimate the dangers of casting a big fly in an adverse wind. I have hooked myself in the ear and had a fly rattle unexpectedly against my sunglasses. Such frightening moments can be avoided by casting over the 'wrong' shoulder or altering one's position in the water.

You will lose nothing by moving along the dam if you wish. You *could* come across a feeding fish sticking to a fixed territory. When you have made your last cast in a chosen spot, try this trick. Instead of retrieving line by hand, reel it in a few turns of the reel handle at a time. It's extraordinary how often a trout will grab a fly so reeled, and it does force you to fish the lure slowly right back to your rod tip.

Nothing doing after a full hour? Why, I once fished six days on a famous water without a touch, and only had one trout of less than $1\frac{3}{4}$lb on the seventh! I admit the same reservoir gave me three brace of trout averaging $1\frac{3}{4}$lb in little over an hour on another, happier occasion. As I've said, it's rather like salmon fishing, for you never know when the mood of the fish will change. When they start taking freely you can equate reservoir trout with fresh-run sea trout.

Oh, a marvellous pull! Listen to that line sizzling through the water as your fish heads for the shallows at the opposite end of the reservoir! He must have hooked himself well and truly and that jump means you've become attached to a plump rainbow trout. Down he goes again, this time moving parallel to the dam. I'd say he took the best part of fifteen yards of line but he's calming down. These chaps, however, do go on fighting with real tenacity, and they are apt to get a second, third and fourth wind after you think you have them beaten.

What a beautiful fish, as silvery as a fresh-run sea trout, but with that lovely pink and mauve sheen down his flanks. At 1lb 5oz he's nothing to be ashamed of on this water. Your fish of the season, in fact. You'll find him quite the best eating of any of your trout this season, too.

Try again in the same place. Unlike brownies, rainbow trout have a shoaling instinct and sometimes you can take advantage of it. I've seen a dozen glorious rainbows promenading along the surface picking off smuts just like a shoal of dace. Mark you, catching dace is easier!

Nothing doing? Lunch then, and a keen watch on the water for the first signs of a rise. It ought to be starting any time now. And while we eat I can talk about some of my reservoir days. Flat calms always trouble me, yet I see from my fishing diary many good fish were taken under such conditions. Generally they grabbed lures fished deep and at a distance.

But the wildest days have been the most exciting. I mean the days when near-gales blew and the waves rolled like surf on to the banks. Bright lures dragged across the tops of the waves have produced some lovely fish on such days. And I've bobbed about in a boat in considerable 'seas' and brought trout up to nymphs and surface flies. They make very exciting swirls on the water, sometimes only a yard from the side of the boat. But more about boats later, now let's get back to work. I've just seen several back fins cutting the wavelets off our shore. Obviously a rise is beginning.

Head for that little promontory further along the bank. It will enable you to reach well out over the line of the feeding fish. Try and cast your flies straight out and allow the breeze and the wave to put a slightly belly in your line. This movement, combined with your steady retrieve, should be attractive to the trout.

A fish has just risen thirty yards down wind of you. Again! This time ten yards nearer. Strip in your line and prepare to cast over his course. I always believe in casting to individual risers unless the fish are moving in positive shoals.

That was a pluck, wasn't it—and you had the will-power and sense not to strike. Continue retrieving at the same speed, accelerating only when you have to lift the flies from the water. He didn't come again. Too bad. One of the fussy ones.

Did you see that rise? He must have swum almost under the rod tip. Whip the flies over him quickly and draw them back almost on the surface to make him dash at them. You have to react quickly to these cruising trout. Fumble the cast and they are out of range in no time.

That fish obviously didn't like the whole cast, half a dozen yards of line and a shower of spray descending on him. My fault for hurrying you. Let's unravel the tangle, calm down and ignore the next few risers: let us, in fact, be content to cast steadily over the same area of water and wait for a trout to come to the flies.

Sure enough one did. No rainbow this but a sturdy ¾lb brownie which liked the look of your little Zulu an inch or two under the surface. A rod bender but not a line taker, not more than a yard or so anyway.

Now I'm going to leave you to it for a while and take a walk. Keep on fishing, and shout if you hook a three-pounder. . . .

How have you done? Touched four fish and failed to hook any of them. Perhaps they saw or heard too much of you. When fish start the tweaking approach you must try various little manœuvres to hook them. Try fishing the flies faster, try smaller flies, try a finer cast, even try (but cautiously) nearly pointing the rod point down the line, hitting any suggestion of a tweak.

It looks as if the wind is going to fail us. A pity, because I like a breath of air to blow the sedges across the water at dusk, assuming there are going to be some about. It also helps to conceal your casting during that irritating period when the trout are drooling about after midge, smut and other microscopic life. They seem to suck midge larvae and spinners off the surface film on these occasions with utter disregard for anything you show them. Greasing your cast down to the last few inches and putting up the smallest, blackest, thinnest tied fly in your box is the only method of attack likely to succeed; unless you want to revert to lure fishing.

Let's walk back across the dam and up the bank near the fishing hut. It doesn't leave so far to go when we've finished and I don't anticipate many fish moving while the sun is still so high in the sky.

Take off both droppers on your nymph cast and change the tail fly for something on the lines suggested. That tiny Alder may do, but let me snip its hackles down with the scissors. Run a hint of line grease right along the cast, only leaving the final four inches untouched. In this game you should try and place your fly in the area in which an individual fish has chosen to rise. When there's no wind to direct their feed and everything is lying slack in the surface scum any movement you impart to a floating line and cast would be bound to scare cruising trout. So you fish your smut as if it was a surface fly, letting it sink through the surface film very slowly indeed and giving it scarcely a twitch of life. I have rarely done much good with surface fly under these conditions. The trout may move in any direction. You may see a nose come up a yard from your fly and confidently anticipate the next rise will be to your fly: usually he rises two yards further away instead!

I advise greasing the cast and holding the fly as close to the surface as possible because that's where all the moving and possibly takeable trout are.

There are some willows leaning over the water further along this bank. Always look for such places and a possibly hungry trout cruising near them in difficult conditions. Watch very carefully for a rise you can reach and drop the fly into the rings of rising trout as quickly as possible. Thereafter, watch the end of the cast for a bulging rise just underwater or a quick pull indicating a take.

Concentrate, now, on that trout close in and possibly coming your way. He's risen twice, thirty yards away, but it's not worth splashing your way towards him and causing a disturbance. Cast your little fly in his direction and hope for the best.

An instant response, which was enough to tighten your line to the rod tip; but that was a quick trout, too quick for a strike, and not the one we saw rise either.

No, they're tricky tonight. Put your hand in the water and

you'll know why. Feels lukewarm doesn't it? Cold air on warm water doesn't suit fly-taking fish: another generalisation, but almost invariably true when the temperature drop is sudden as it was this evening.

There are now quite a few rising trout within reach but they seem to delight in turning aside from your fly at the last moment. Soon it will be dusk, and by the regulations time to stop fishing. Most reservoirs have to be cleared of anglers an hour or an hour and a half after sunset. Just as well, otherwise they might be cleared of most of their best fish.

You had better do the traditional thing for the last half-hour—and don't confuse my use of the word traditional with something old-fashioned. Fishing two large flies at dusk is a time-honoured and very killing method on reservoirs and lakes. Alas, there's no sedge about tonight but if you pick up the heavier rod you will observe I have tied on a Worm fly as dropper, leaving the Alexandra at the tail.

The Worm fly, or a Palmer, is the pattern I have most confidence in at this stage of the day and in this position on the cast. Fish it close in and let it dribble across the surface before lifting to re-cast. Even in a flat calm such as this you may goad trout into slashing at the fly, providing your casts are made gently. The dimmer the light gets, the closer trout can be expected to come towards the bank. On my favourite Devon reservoir, where no wading is allowed, I have caught trout less than a rod's length out in the last few minutes of the day, and done it standing upright, though dead still.

Unfortunately, without a few natural sedges to encourage them, the trout here appear to have stayed on their smut diet. Rises have become fewer and in a moment you must make your last cast or we shall be prosecuted! So try a good long one, let both flies sink deeply and then walk quietly out of the water with the rod on your shoulder before reeling up. This produces a different action and may induce a trout to take even if it has seen the flies before.

Bang! That one followed right in before deciding the Worm fly was too juicy to refuse. He's not large so don't stand on ceremony but walk back another yard or two and beach him.

Trout don't fight particularly hard in the dusk, largely because they can't see enough to get really frightened. I'd say this one wasn't over $\frac{3}{4}$lb, but that gives you a leash averaging almost 1lb for the day, which sounds good. That successful bit of fly fishing certainly was easy.

CHAPTER EIGHT

TROUT: *Highland Lake—Surface Fly Fishing*

THEORY

THE word 'highland' mustn't be taken too literally. To many British anglers it means the hill lochs of Scotland lying a thousand or two thousand feet up in precipitous hill clefts. These are truly highland lochs, but even Scotland has its lowland-type waters; and Wales and the West Country have reservoirs or lakes whose characteristics are principally 'highland'. In fact, there are reservoirs such as Clatworthy in Somerset and Wistlandpound in Devon which are more typically highland than lowland; and the South West Devon reservoirs close to Dartmoor lie round the 800ft contour and combine something of the characteristics of both.

Generally I would say any lake over 1,000ft is certainly a highland one; very often it may only be half as high and still fish like a highland water. If it is deep and acid and breeds and maintains only small trout it is of highland type. True, some of these lakes contain very large trout which feed either on small trout, char or some other indigenous fish; they are occasionally caught on fly, but normally taken on deep-fished spinners and therefore need no mention in this book.

Lowland reservoirs contain rich feeding and produce fat trout of high average weight. In most highland waters the living is frugal by comparison. Consequently, you will find a freer-rising, smaller breed of trout in the latter. Since the takeable trout in my local reservoirs average 10oz and 14oz—according to which of the two favourite waters they come from—and these results are quite common in many similar reservoirs and lakes, there's not much to grumble about. Certainly a day on a highland water is more likely to produce incidents than the same day on the plain; but the fish will be smaller and less tasty.

The depth of some highland waters, naturally or artificially set in the clefts of the hills, is itself an ally to the fly fisherman, especially to the surface fly fisherman. In these lakes there may be precious little natural water fly—which peters out in depths of more than 12 to 15ft—but the trout (like those of acid, moorland brooks) will be on the look-out for anything dropping off high banks or out of the trees along the water's edge. Small, hungry trout which rise freely offer more entertainment than the portly two-pounders of lowland waters which rise twice a week!

Now to boats. I prefer bank fishing, but many far better anglers swear by boat fishing while I swear at it. After several tough and fishless days on the bank I enjoy going afloat for a change, but I do it more for the sake of variety than for sheer fish catching. But to be honest, in large lakes of any sort, particularly those of Scotland and Ireland, boats are virtually essential to reach the best fly fishing areas which are on the shallows, around islands and similar areas inaccessible from the shore. On the smaller hill waters of England and Wales they are not so necessary. Banking is mainly static. Boating gives you command of a tremendous area of water, providing there is breeze enough to keep you on the move, and casting is much easier work for you throw only a short line.

I look upon a boat as an occasional ally, but a tiresome one. Athough it's fun to be out on the waves, bobbing up and down with a clean breeze on your cheeks, much valuable fishing time will be wasted unless you have a gillie or a good friend at the oars. It isn't easy to function efficiently alone as angler *and* boatman.

Many boats are equipped with outboard motors; smelly, noisy but efficient at getting you to a drift—which is the line you allow the boat to wallow along before the breeze. If you step into a boat whose power is the traditional oar and muscle, you will need to be fit for a full day's fly fishing on a windy lake! Whatever happens, see that you have enough fuel to power your outboard, plus a spare plug and the wherewithal to unscrew the existing one if needs be. And ensure that the oars and rowlocks are fixed in some way to the boat to prevent mishaps.

Boats drift at considerable speed before a brisk wind, especially the really 'seaworthy', high-built type. The slower they go the better for fly fishing, so a sea anchor—which is a funnel-shaped piece of canvas attached to some ten yards of rope—is a useful piece of equipment to keep down the rate of knots. And boats do have one great advantage. They frighten trout less than wading anglers; so much so that trout will often rise under the rod tip as you drift along. They are also the best platform for fishing the surface fly in a slight ripple, or a big wave. Sunk flies should drag, in some way, to be effective; surface flies should sit without any drag, the sedge excepted.

Very short rods can be employed from a boat, but I prefer at least a nine-footer because it keeps the flies just a little farther from you when they are being lifted. The nine-footer will flip out a greater length of line and, if a hooked trout dives under the boat, can be dipped sharply down into the water to clear the cast from the keel—a hazardous moment when the owner of a 6ft 6in toy rod might find himself in trouble. So tackle need not be changed over for the highland water, and because so short a line is generally cast from a boat—a relaxing business—there's no need to call on the heavy rod which casts your lures in richer waters.

Surface fly can be a most successful method in any still water, even on the most dour of lowland reservoirs. But it comes into its own on the higher, deeper lakes where food is rather scarce. I've said already that I do not like glassy calm conditions for fishing the fly up top, for trout then see and hear too much. When there is anything from a ripple to a wave the chances are best.

Drag, that old enemy of the river, causes trouble on still waters too. Try fishing a surface fly from the bank with the wind in any direction except absolutely facing you! But sit in a boat which is drifting along with the wind, drop your surface fly a few yards in front of it and you will soon see how the fly rides naturally on the surface as your craft bears down upon it. Trout moving up wind towards the drift of the boat will see a small fly riding perkily towards them, and no nylon cast or ripples from drag.

Basically, there are two methods of fishing floating fly on still water. They are the normal way, casting as one does on a river but allowing the fly to sit on the surface as long as possible, and by dapping. The lattter differs from the dapping already described although the principle is the same. Long, light rods of up to 16ft or more are used and between the short cast and the line a length of floss line is tied to catch the breeze and swing the fly ahead of the boat, allowing it to trip across the surface. This is how mayfly, natural and artificial, is fished on the great lakes of Ireland; it is also a useful method for daddy-longlegs fishing anywhere, or the sedge rise.

A surface fly does not need to be any larger just because some lakes appear so vast. There is a temptation to use larger patterns but this should be resisted unless you have to fish in a big wave. Some dapping flies are tied large and bushy and they can be very successful, though I consider small patterns, say sizes 14 up to 10, the best all-rounders. Patterns need not vary much. I've found my Pheasant Tails, Alders and Palmers or Red Quill, a killing enough bunch. Pick flies capable of sitting up on the water for a long time and keep for river work those patterns forever becoming waterlogged.

Watching a small dry fly from a boat demands a high degree of concentration. It is essential to see your trout rise, or he will never be yours, and this can test the finest eyesight. Timing the strike is a matter of practice, practice, practice. The bigger the trout the slower he rises and you must develop the ability to watch a large mouth gulp down your fly without striking wildly and pulling it out before the trout closes his jaws. In a river, most trout will take fly quickly, regaining their feeding position promptly. In a lake, the trout are cruising, at times almost like whales going through plankton with their mouths open! Sometimes you will find yourself in a near calm casting to trout which are up and feeding avidly in all directions. These would certainly be faster takers, and a strike immediately the fly was taken the best policy.

Very often two anglers will fish from a boat, the gillie or a third angler being at the oars on the centre seat. In this case they should, ideally, both be casting with their outside hand, left-handed if you are seated on the gillie's left. Casting with the 'wrong' arm isn't difficult, but striking and managing the first rush of a fish may be. Therefore if you stick to right-arm casting what-

Space and solitude. Loch Cama with Suilven on the skyline

A March salmon from the River Exe

Grayling are handsome fish

ever your position, remind yourself constantly of the potential danger of your flies to the gillie.

Where you will fish the floating fly on a lake depends on your knowledge of it, or your intuition and water sense if it's an unknown water. I enjoy drifts close in along high banks where trees, bushes or ferns overhang the water's edge. Here both you and the trout can depend on surface feed when the wind is right—coming off-shore. I also look closely at areas fringed by tall grass or rushes from which sedge-type flies often emerge. Incidentally, ferns and grasses in hill country, and particularly Wales, produce a wonderful beetle rise in the summer, so carry a few Coch-y-Bondhu patterns in your fly tin ready to take advantage.

Finally, remember once again that it's the fly on the water that takes most fish. Don't keep it waggling about in the breeze, leave it on the water as long as possible after each cast. With this uppermost in your mind, come with me to a Welsh mountain lake, any lake will do, and share a boat on a pleasant June morning.

PRACTICE

Early June—a lovely time of year in the hills. The new ferns are a fresh green and, nearer the edge of this lake, bluebells still provide an exciting foreground display. Conifers grow up the slopes from the eastern shore of the lake, which is about half a mile long and less than a quarter of a mile wide.

Much of the water is deep: one glance at the steep hill slopes plunging into it tells you so. Several small streams race down over boulder-strewn courses into the top end of the lake, and one leaves it at the lower end, falling very steeply indeed for several hundred yards before levelling up and reaching the next lake where your car had to be left. And there's the boathouse, a couple of hundred yards along, tucked in that little bay.

This is a water whose trout are small but free-rising. A half-pounder is a monster and a pounder the event of a season, perhaps several seasons. The breeze is cutting through a gap in the hills to our right and funnelling on up the lake towards the top end. A good direction because it will give us a long drift parallel with the steep, tree-lined bank. If it does not get up any more it will give us a valuable, slow drift and it should not be too hard to row back against it. If it peters out altogether fishing will be difficult, but I don't think that's likely. Up here there's usually some ripple over the water surface on the hottest days, though the hills do tend to change the direction of some breezes unexpectedly.

Hand me your waterproofs, net, food and drink, and I'll stow them in the bows. While I'm making things shipshape you can set up your tackle—the light 9ft rod and a light cast with one small dry fly; any fly with a black or brown hackle goes well here.

Right! I've stowed all the gear out of the way of our feet. The net stays beside us just in case we hook a monster, though I'm certain we shall not. Place your rod carefully along one side of the boat, taking special care to see that the tip is tucked out of harm's way. I'll take the oars and push gently out. Sit still, and stay seated at all times in a boat until every other occupant has been given warning that you intend to move. The average rowing boat takes a good deal of capsizing but it happens every year, and drownings result. You can swim, so I know you are not likely to panic in emergency; but I think any non-swimmer would be well advised to wear a life-jacket or have a lifebuoy at hand.

You've suggested with admirable deference that a team of three nymphs might do better than a single surface fly. Quite right! But you're here to practise with a small floater and, believe me, you'll get plenty of fun. Look along the shore beyond this bay, you will certainly see some rises.

I've brought the boat far enough out to clear the point of the bay. In front of us as we drift gently, bow turned towards the shore, is a good quarter mile of fishing. It's rough country for a bank angler and sheer de-luxe idleness in this comfortable craft! No stumbling and sweating through brambles and ferns to reach the water; no catching up of the fly on our back casts; no carrying of tackle and lunch parcels, including full bottles; these are among the advantages of the boat.

In this light breeze a very occasional touch on the oars will keep us on a straight course. Your weight on the bow seat will keep her nose down a little and also help slow the drift. Don't attempt a long line, there's no need for it. Drop your fly quietly two or three rod lengths ahead and pick up loose line with your free hand as if you were collecting it on a river. The fly sits tight until the boat drifts down on it, of course. You must not move it, but as you begin to lift for another cast by all means trip it across the surface in the hope of raising a fish at the very last moment. Try to flick off all the moisture on your fly with one brisk false cast and then . . . out it goes again.

If you do notice a rise towards the shore which means shifting your position and casting back over my head, *tell* me first and take extra care. If you see a fish move in front of me, *don't* be tempted to steal a march, or, inevitably, our flies will clash in knotty combat!

Boating demands some discipline. You will find plenty of trout in front of you and I don't think on lakes like this your bag will be any the heavier for a series of wild casts all around the boat. Another point: when drifting fast towards a rough, rocky shore, never be tempted into a few reckless final casts. Pull clear in good time. Boats are expensive and yet rarely treated with half the care we lavish on the tin cans sold to us as cars. If an outboard motor is fitted, always be sure you are in water deeper than its propeller before starting it. Outboards cost money, too!

First blood to you! That trout wasn't scared of the boat, was he? He took the fly as you lifted it and put up a most energetic performance for a mature and weighty fish all of 3oz. Dry your fly quickly, there are several rising fish in the area we are approaching.

The hands of my watch point to midday exactly. I don't think times are particularly important on an overstocked lake of this type, where trout may rise all day, but it could be that the fish will come enthusiastically to the fly for a while and then lose interest; or maybe we are in the right place at the right time.

Second blood to me—no, he's off. Ah, another had the fly before you could say 'Titanic Troutlets'. I've beaten you by an ounce.

Don't thrash about, don't get so excited. Relax and drop your fly quietly in the rings of the nearest riser. If he doesn't have it, one of his pals will. Splendid. We're both playing small trout and the net won't need to be wetted for this pair. These fish are rather like the trout of the Dulas brook, and a whole lot easier to catch.

I'm a firm believer in making a bag while conditions are right. There will be plenty of time to admire the scenery once this rise is over; and if the rise continues I should be quite happy to set myself a limit—a dozen, a score or two dozen fish, for example—and then lay off. There's all the difference in the world between a sensible bag and a sackful.

I spoke too soon. We appear to have drifted through the free-rising fish area into a blank patch. If we don't rise a trout in the next fifty yards I'm going to row back, swinging the boat in a semi-circle well away from the shore until we are at our starting point.

No good—here goes then. While I'm rowing, tie on a flashy sunk lure of suitable size for your cast and pay it out twenty yards behind the boat. Put down your rod with most of the top joint projecting over the stern and ensure that the reel handle is unobstructed. This is trolling or trailing your fly, unskilled and considered unsporting on some waters. Its advantage, where rules and moral laws permit, is that it will frequently stir a good trout on a bad day. If they ignore a trolled fly the trout are unlikely to be interested in any other method. But never troll unless you are certain the practice will offend no one.

Want a bet on the chances of your rod tip suddenly dipping? We're almost back to the fishful area and at the rate I'm rowing your fly could well have sunk deep enough to interest one of the monsters.

Whew! There it goes, and how you jumped for the rod handle. He seems to have hooked himself, but keep a good bend in the rod and ensure the hold pulls in over the barb. Don't worry—I'm ready with the net for this monster. Got him. He weighs 10oz and you won't catch anything larger today.

Now tie your surface fly on again and we'll drift through the killing area. . . . Not bad. Another brace apiece and several more splashy rises which amounted to nothing. We were obviously a little late starting. When we've lunched and looked our fill at the views I shall try a new drift on the far shore. . . .

Ready for more? Off we go, straight across the lake and then a drift towards the top end, which will take us past the mouths of two of the bright little feeder streams. The breeze will be sufficient to drift us gradually in towards the bank and I shall then take the oars and keep you at the right casting distance from the shore. This side of the lake is a little rougher and more exposed, and some cloud has built up in the last hour. Put up a slightly larger, darker fly.

Notice how the breeze is sweeping diagonally along the shore. I'm going to try and hold the boat square to it, using the oars to keep it a constant distance from the shore. I want you to cast your floating fly as close to the bank as possible. The water is deep close in except at the mouths of the streams where gravel deposits have formed; good spots for trout on any water. We are going to move faster here, so keep gathering line and make more frequent casts. Watch your fly closely; watch for a swirl or that glint of gold under the surface if you lose sight of the fly in the 'surf'.

Third cast, a rise; and the next cast too. Wonder why you didn't hook them, or him? Throw closer to the bank where that tiny rill comes in. Yes, he was there. I'm holding the boat here to give you another cast in that spot. Missed him. Let's move on.

It's exhilarating, and not too serious a day's fishing. I should say you've had your dozen trout, and if you had fished a team of three nymphs you would surely have accounted for over a score of these eager little chaps. My suggestion to end the day is a walk back to the car and a try with the sedge on the lower lake at dusk. It's full early in the season for sedge, but something may appear. We shall fish from the bank down there. . . .

Here we are. Tie on a bushy Palmer whose brown hackles run from the eye of a No 12 hook down to its bend. This gives the impression of a fat, leggy insect with large shimmering wings—we hope! The breeze is still on the water, and it's a grand warm one. If my favourite big red sedges start scuttering out from the bay where those rushes are growing you should have some fun. Trout here are fewer and larger than in the upper lake.

The sun has gone, and much of its glow has left the sky. There are a number of rising trout, yes, and a sedge or two now. See them? Monstrous, dark brown creatures fluttering sometimes, and sometimes sitting still on the water. There are two within your casting range. If they are taken, cast your fly in front of the line you believe the trout is following—it will be directly up or down wind here—and pull it gently back towards you, making it set up a riffle on the water. There is no better method of attracting a still water trout to the sedge. Alternatively, allow your sedge to sit on the water or fish it just submerged with some seductive shoreward movements.

There's a trout! He's taken both naturals so be quick to offer him your version. See how he dashed at it. The line tightened and all you had to do was lift the rod and hit him.

Sedge rises are seldom lengthy affairs, and I find they often cease before all daylight has gone. Tonight is no exception. Wait, though—here's a last-moment scrounger of a trout rising his way towards you. Cast towards him, and follow round if you get no response, chasing his tail if necessary! Happily he saw your fly, and wanted it. That's your brace of half-pounders and a foretaste of many a splendid sedge rise in future seasons.

CHAPTER NINE

SEA TROUT: *Day Fishing*

THEORY

THINK of sea trout without that magic word 'sea' (which gives them their lovely silver colour, their strength, their flavour on the table). They are, in fact, trout which for reasons as yet unexplained choose to migrate seawards in the same way as young salmon, and at roughly the same stage in their development, returning in shoals to most of our rivers during the summer months.

Sea trout particularly favour tributaries or small rivers, which accounts for the excellence of many rivers in the West Country, Wales and the west coast of Scotland. Where native trout run small, as they do in most of our acid western rivers, the presence of sea trout is a blessing. I defy any angler normally obliged to fish for half-pounders and lesser fry to say his heart does not beat quicker at the sight of a shoal of two to three-pound sea trout lying quietly in a clear pool, with a five-pounder as vanguard!

Sea trout are no fools when they grow large. Unlike salmon which make only one spawning trip, or two at most (third-time spawners are recorded but rare) these wary fish will continue to run their rivers year after year, living ten years or more if they escape all the perils that nature and man put in their way.

Generally the larger sea trout enter our rivers first, from March onwards, and the odd few monsters of 10lb and upwards may be caught like salmon. As the season advances their numbers increase and their size decreases. The fresher they are from the sea the easier it is to tempt them to take a fly. They are likely to take with zest and their fight is unforgettable. Earlier I compared them with rainbow trout; they are much livelier than big brown trout or small salmon.

Sea trout become more and more difficult to catch, and begin to look like ordinary brown trout, when they have been in a river some weeks. The cock fish start to look like kelts (a term applied to salmon and sea trout after spawning and until their return to sea). Treat big, new sea trout like salmon and the old stagers as wily trout. Offer the former large, silvery flies and treat the latter to trout patterns. Fish bigger and brighter flies the closer you are to the sea.

Sea trout, unlike salmon, will run up rivers even in low water and make their way into the pools through a shrunken series of trickles if necessary. They *will* take surface fly, but it is seldom the best method. It can, however, be very entertaining at times if you care to experiment.

For reasons unexplained, sea trout in the West Country, Wales and parts of the north, are very hard to catch during daylight. Yet in many Scottish rivers and lakes, and in Ireland too, they are easily caught by day. This applies particularly in lakes. From every point of view, it will pay you to seek local knowledge when going sea-trout fishing, and, above all, make a careful reconnaissance of your water.

Sea trout are not difficult to find in clear rivers and, as in trouting, you will succeed if you keep out of sight and drop your fly on target quietly. The first fish may come easily, but others in the shoal soon appreciate there's trouble about and start getting nervy. This is one of the most difficult features about low-water, sea-trout fishing; in high water or a dirty spate it doesn't matter very much and a succession of them can be caught in favourable places.

Unless you are very lucky, you will soon rate the sea trout way ahead of both brown trout and salmon in terms of intelligence. Master your fly rod, though, and you will be one up on the spinners and wormers of this wicked world when more rivers become 'fly only' to conserve the fish.

Why tackle should be advertised as sea-trout strength, length or size, is a perplexing point. When you remember they are trout and scale your tackle accordingly you are on the right track. How many of us catch 10lb sea trout regularly? If we did, it would be wise to use light salmon tackle. Most of the sea trout taken in

Britain are 3lb and under. Where they run larger, there is no need to fear them on trout rods, especially if they are hooked in big, open rivers or lakes.

Fish for sea trout as you fished for the brown trout of the lowland reservoir, with the light 9ft rod for normal work and the heavier rod, say up to 10ft, where long casting with a big lure is necessary. Your reels, lines and casts too, can be just the same. The floating line is most useful, especially when sea trout are on the feed and moving about for fly, and the sunk line is equally useful when the fish are lying deep and need their noses bumping with a lure. By day, casts and flies ought to resemble those in use for trout, unless the fish are *very* large and fresh or there is a spate running down.

Where do you look for sea trout? Not, normally, in places where you would expect salmon or trout which prefer faster water and tend to work their way into the rough heads of the pools or hover in strong streams. No, sea trout opt for the slack water, well covered by trees, bushes or boulders, where there is a respectable depth to protect them. Their liking for the slack water poses an immediate problem: how to fish a fly without arousing their suspicion. Long casting, combined with deep wading or creeping and crawling, may be the answer; and a high wind setting up a real riffle on the quiet river surface can be a godsend.

I think it advisable to stick to one fly on a cast for daytime fishing—except in 'easy' conditions such as gale or flood fishing—and it should be a sunk fly. Sometimes dry fly is useful. When there is a tinge of colour in the water sea trout may rise just like brownies. The chances are, of course, always better with the small fish. At dusk, too, the dry fly may prove a killer. Try a big sedge pattern over the gentle rises you spot on a good length of sea trout water, and be prepared for fireworks! And if dusk fishing is good, night fishing is invariably better still. I shall couple the two together in the next section.

Spate fishing may be exciting if you are fishing at the right moment. Knowledge of your river is of great value. If you can march confidently down to the top of a long rapid where travelling fish might be expected to pause for a breather after fighting their way up a torrent, if you can recall a quiet stretch of normally shallow water broken up by a few large stones, if you have access to the river immediately above a weir or waterfall, then you will have a chance of catching sea trout while a flood drops away.

Fish a lure or a team of flies, and remember sea trout will take in peat or 'porridge' water which looks virtually unfishable—and would be unfishable for salmon. You can relax and stand up to your fishing in times of spate. Even then, don't expect to take sea trout under your rod tip. The water is never as dirty from beneath as it appears looking down at it.

Fishing for sea trout in low water can be the very devil. If you approach a shoal from below you will not alarm them until you hook a fish, and occasionally several may be taken at intervals, but your fly must cover only the stragglers at the rear and usually they are the smallest fish.

Don't forget dapping where the river banks suit the method. Many sea trout lie in midstream and cannot be reached with a dapped fly, but observation and cautious reconnaissance will teach you the best places. I rate this business of water spotting top priority for sea trout fishermen. Sea trout are not necessarily here today *and* tomorrow. Be sure your water holds them before rushing out to fish.

When you hook a sea trout it will usually be lively and a strong, thrusting fighter. The larger fish tend to run swiftly downstream and then back up, often coming out of the water in a wild jump at the end of their runs. They *must* be allowed to run freely, you check them (like reservoir trout) not by brute force but by *easing* off all pressure. When their first wind has gone you may safely start pulling them about and stopping any dangerous short runs towards rocks, submerged branches and other obstacles. The small fish, school peal, sewen or herling as they are known respectively in the West Country, Wales and the North, often flurry on the surface and exhaust themselves quicker than brown trout of similar size.

Finally, a word on flies. I should not like to be without Mallard and Claret (sizes 8 to 14) Teal Blue and Silver, the Haslam and some sort of two or three-hook lure or tube fly on Elverine lines. These, together with ordinary trout flies, are sufficient to start with. Buy some double-hook patterns, for deep fishing, and have some of your flies tied as tube flies. Tubes have become remarkably popular in the last decade. Their advantage is lightness, good 'travel' through the water and the fact that they are fished with small trebles whose hooking and holding power are superior to the traditional single-hook fly. The size of the treble hook is easily varied, for the nylon cast is just threaded through the tube and knotted to it, thus:

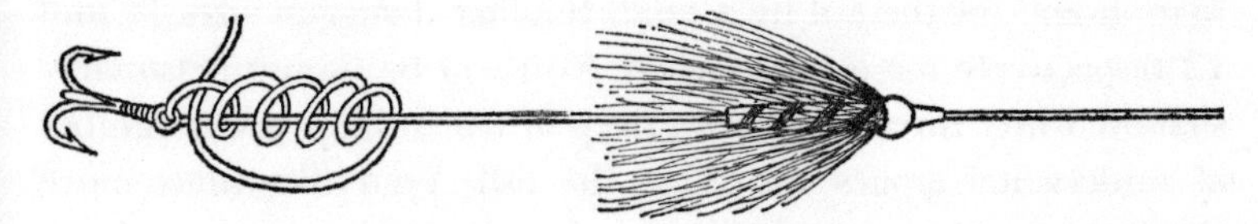

Tube fly, treble hook and knot

And now to the banks of a river in the West Country for a week-end's sea-trout fishing.

PRACTICE

Here we are on the Devonshire Torridge. The river flows through a dramatic landscape of steep, well-wooded combes, but its flow is steady and it is rarely gin clear. It is not as dashing as the Dart or Teign in the south of the county, nor as broad and slow as the lower Exe. But it is an ideal size for a sea-trout river. Where it cannot be covered from the bank or shallows, it offers safe wading.

July is not the best of months for the fly fisherman, unless he turns to sea trout. At this stage of the season there are bound to be peal—as Devonians call their sea trout—in the lower and middle reaches of this lovely river. Not all the big chaps have gone upstream, and more than a sprinkling of the school fish will have come up to join them.

This stretch of river is four or five feet deep in low water, and from the high right bank we shall see some of its secrets. There they are! A brace of salmon and a couple of dozen sea trout. Further downstream the river disappears into a tunnel of trees; there is a long and lovely glide which holds sea trout for a couple of hundred yards or more, a large rock outcrop which shelters the salmon, and then the weir. We shall be lucky if we make a kill before dusk, but there's no harm in trying down the fastest stretch of water where the river glides into its leafy tunnel. After that you might consider other tactics, dapping for instance.

I think you'd better put up the heavier rod but stick to the floating line. Tie on a trout-strength cast tapered down to 3lb b.s., and, if you can manage, let it be the best part of four yards long. One fly or two? It doesn't much matter. I think a dropper on the cast is an advantage on the whole, so put on a Pheasant Tail nymph and for the tail fly a small Butcher. I suggest sizes 14 and 12 respectively for a trial period. You will be fishing reasonably shallow water three to five feet deep in which there are a number of underwater stones sheltering the fish. Your flies must move slowly to avoid undue disturbance from the nylon cast; too large a size would sink deep and become snagged. Wade in quietly.

This is downstream fishing with sunk fly. Before starting, ensure that both flies and the entire cast sink. Because this is a warm, sunny midsummer day and the river is low and clear, you must try and throw as long a line as possible, drawing the flies as gently as possible when the slight current has pulled them in the customary arc across the holding water. Movement of the flies is always essential.

Did you notice that slight 'bulge' in the water a foot behind your tail fly? Obviously you moved a fish of some sort, it could have been one of the many sea trout in this reach. Rest him for a minute—and I mean the full sixty seconds—before trying the same cast again. Hard luck. That fish must have been scared in some way by the first cast.

You've been struggling along for almost an hour now, no doubt feeling just as hot and frustrated as you look. So why not move upstream with me to another pleasant spot and try a surface fly with the light 9ft rod? I've put the rod together ready for action. You'll need the reel with the floating line, of course.

Tie on a fairly large Tup, say a No 10 which looks even larger than it really is thanks to its voluminous hackles. An improbably large dry fly like this will sometimes bring up an inquisitive sea trout even in the middle of the hottest days. Mark you, it's never a certainty, just a faint possibility.

This pool is best covered from the left bank and shallow side of the river. There is a gravel shoal which narrows the river here and some current under the far bank which rises vertically six feet; trees cover it like a series of umbrellas. Sea trout appreciate its three-star comforts. If you kneel in the shallows and creep gradually upstream there will be room to throw your tremendous Tup across and up ahead of you. Fish it exactly as you would fish for brown trout, but remember your quarry know more about enemies like you than the local quarter-pounders. Don't lift your fly off the water until it has drifted at least five yards downstream of your 'target' area. Don't cast too frequently because even a 'thistledown' landing will not go unnoticed by the sea trout.

That was a thoroughly good effort, and I thought when that rise came you would be into the fish. I don't believe you did anything wrong, the sea trout may have bumped your fly for fun without actually mouthing it. It looked like the rise of a fish between 1lb and 2lb.

The shallow above this pool is only likely to contain parr and the odd small brownies, so you might as well give up for a while. I suggest an early evening meal and a leisurely return to the river for the dusk rise. Brown trout rise best just as the sun goes down. Sea trout move later still, starting in the dusk and normally rising best during the first hour of darkness.

Below the pool you fished with surface fly this afternoon is a long stretch of very slack water. From the left bank you cast diagonally downstream trying to drop your two sunk flies as near to the well-wooded far bank as possible. Retrieve them towards your own bank by gently drawing the line. Use the cast you tried earlier in the day and, to make casting easier, snip off the extra couple of feet from its top end, re-tying the loop where it joins the line.

As the light goes the sea trout will start to feed, or cruise around taking a 'breather'. Some may be anxious to run upstream. Fish on the move like this are bound to be an easier proposition than the inert shoals at midday. You may notice some heavy swirls in the water where it is deep, dark and well shaded by overhanging tree branches. You may be startled by the sudden whirring of a leaping sea trout's tail, followed by the heavy splash as he hits the water again. Watch for the bats, listen for the first owl : then it is sea-trout time !

You are making your casts slowly and gently: a good point. Try casting a little squarer to the far bank, remembering the lack of current here and the need to fish that little Butcher well up in the water with sufficient movement to make its silver tinsel body flash and attract fish.

He has it! Not a big one but a lively customer. Keep a light strain on him and I think you'll find when his jumping is done he'll turn on his side and come spent to the net. It's easy to see those silvery sides in the gloaming. Grand! You've caught your first sea trout, an ounce or two under 1lb admittedly, but sizeable. Now you have about ten minutes' light left before packing up. Wade on down as far as you dare and gradually extend your line over to the far bank. It's all excellent water.

You knew all about that rise in a twinkling. A savage wrench at the rod top which bent it down to the butt, line torn away through your fingers and off the reel—yards of it! Keep in touch. He's made his downstream run and will now probably come up again, accelerating when you get a strain on him. Be patient. Sea trout are often lightly hooked and their mouths, when very fresh run, are inclined to be softer than those of brown trout of the same size.

This fish has jumped only once, but he's capable of repeating the performance on a tight line if you try hustling him. Play him firmly until he turns over on his side exhausted, then draw him over your net with one easy movement.

Not so easy to lift up that one was it? Looks a good 2lb to me but you'll have to wait until we get the car lights on to see the figures on the spring balance. And if the take of that fish hasn't made you a sea trout addict for life I shall be astonished.

* * *

That prize-winning thunderstorm last night must have kept half Devon awake. It didn't rain very much here but the upper reaches undoubtedly caught it. I went down to the river while you were still asleep and found it filthy and obviously rising. There's no chance of fishing until after lunch when the river should be dropping again.

Floods vary from river to river. The Torridge is not typically moorland and comes down very dirty at times. The Dartmoor rivers like Tavy, Teign and Dart, may run black with peat but still very clear after rain. Salmon don't like peat, or too much colour in the river; but sea trout oblige at times.

Personally, I go down to the river with high hopes when conditions are such that fish are running. There is always a chance that sea trout or salmon will grab a bait when they are pausing for a breather. They are excited by their movement upstream and much more likely to have a snatch at your bait than they would be after a month's rest in some near-stagnant pool. . . .

This pool is not one of my low water favourites. It is deep and sluggish and both banks are high and wooded. It always holds quantities of sea trout but you must wade well across to reach them and they don't like that a bit. However, the river is still a nasty colour this afternoon, and a little higher than I expected, so problems of concealment and cautious casting will not be so alarming. The advantage of this pool in high water is that the normally placid tail end is something of a refuge for fish which have struggled up some hundreds of yards of rough, shallow water. Many of these travellers shoot into the pool and rest briefly before moving on. The last twenty or thirty yards of the pool, where it starts to narrow and speed up into the rapids, is the crucial area.

In these conditions a fairly large, showy fly is an advantage. Sea trout fresh up from the tide will snatch at large mouthfuls; in any case, you want them to see the lure as it moves through the 'fog' underwater. Put up a size 8 Teal Blue and Silver as tail fly and for a dropper try a Haslam a couple of sizes smaller. The cast had better be no finer than 7lb b.s. as there's always the chance of a big sea trout on this river, and a slighter chance (this month) of a salmon.

This beat yielded a sea trout of nearly 10lb in just these conditions a few seasons ago, and fish half that weight are frequently caught.

How do you cast when standing hard up against the right bank which rises a good six to eight feet almost vertically? You have two alternatives. You may cast vertically—instead of extending line behind you, flick it upwards and then forward—or you may fish left-handed, which keeps the back cast clear of the bank providing you aim well downstream.

Try the vertical cast. It's not too difficult and you will find it a very useful style in any similar place. Using it, I've hooked sea trout from a pool with a sheer rock face directly behind me. With so much colour in the river and your excellent background cover you will not need a long line. Flick the flies across and downstream —but more across—and let them swing round steadily, pulling them if they show signs of slowing up under your bank. Sea trout may be resting temporarily in only a foot or so of water. Wade down quietly after half a dozen casts from each stance until you are covering that last, smooth stretch of water where the pool ends.

You've fished it down once, blank. Don't be discouraged. Wade back upstream and start again. You might usefully spend an entire afternoon in one promising place waiting for running fish to arrive.

I've just seen the back fin or tail of a sea trout close under the far bank and almost opposite your starting point. Wade back up a step or two and cast as nearly straight across as you can manage. Make the flies hurry through the turgid water once they're sunk about a foot.

He's taken you. A very silvery, fresh little fish this. Don't let him turn turtle and float out of the pool. Work him round below you and then put enough pressure on to persuade him upstream to the net. If even a small beaten fish goes out of the pool you are fishing then you will have to run after him or risk a loss! He's a good pounder, lightly hooked on the tail fly. He wasn't too lively because he'd been travelling. Lucky for you, because a typical jumper would have freed that slender hook-hold.

Try the same spot exactly. If that fish was in company and they are still resting you may get another or even a whole series. Down goes that rod tip again, and this time the reel is revolving fast enough to frighten you. Is it a monster? No, exactly the same size as your first. Curious how different their fights can be.

That seems to be all here. No miraculous shoal to provide you with continuous sport. Let's move downstream and try a length of steady water which is normally rather too shallow to hold

Nearly 3 lb—a Devon reservoir brown trout in perfect condition

Three Teign sea trout. The best, nearly 4½ lb, was hooked in the tail and took almost ten minutes to land

A moorland river in spring. The angler is fishing sunk fly downstream

sea trout. In this spate they may be hanging about in it. There are some large, well-rounded stones to provide temporary resting places. You can fish this length from dry land as there is a pleasant shingle beach on our side. Don't stand up; kneel a yard or more from the water and expect a pull as your flies move across the centre line of the river which is the deepest portion here.

Don't hesitate to cast your flies almost on top of the boulders you see just above water, or on those whose position you can only guess by the 'riffle' they create on the surface. These are the obvious resting places for fish. Others you will find out by experience. I can tell you, to save your time, that the first fifty yards of this gentle glide is your best hope and the following 100 yards rather too shallow except in much higher floods. That length you can safely ignore, moving on down to a point opposite that venerable old oak where there is, unseen today, a deep depression in the river bed for several yards which may easily hold a resting fish or two. It's known to the initiated as 'The Trough'. A few casts over The Trough and then it will be time to finish.

Here's the oak, and The Trough is between midstream and the far bank, roughly under the end of the branch which is pointing directly at us. It pays to 'hang' the flies in it as long as possible, which means a downstream cast and a long line. As the flies drift towards the taking area, lift the line with an anti-clockwise motion of the rod tip a good yard or more back towards midstream. It's quite possible to do this without moving the cast and flies. It's called 'mending' the line and its purpose is to slow down the sideways or cross-stream track of the flies. It is a common manœuvre in salmon fishing when the fly has so often to be slowed down in a fast current. The illustration overleaf shows how it should look in practice.

See what you can do while I start packing up the oddments.

Look out, man, look out! Stop hauling at the rod. Get your hand away from the reel and run downstream like a terrier after him. I reckon he's almost in the next pool already. Run!

You can't feel anything at all? Well, whatever it was may have turned upstream again, so reel in hurriedly just in case. No, you are broken. Might have been a big sea trout but I believe it was a salmon. If they turn downstream and you go on pulling it

H

merely makes them even more determined to reach the sea in record time. I'm sorry your week-end had to finish like this, but what a thrill while it lasted!

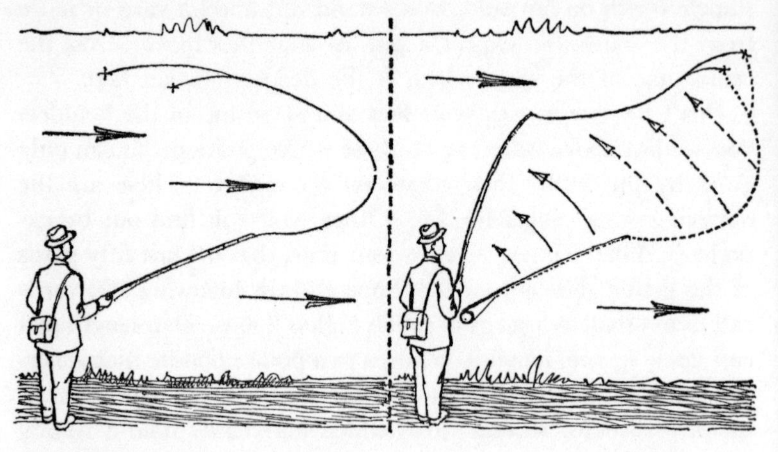

Before mending, current is putting 'U' bend in line; after mending, line is straightened again and fast pull of current on flies ceases

CHAPTER TEN

SEA TROUT: *Night Fishing*

THEORY

NIGHT fishing for sea trout is the most exacting, yet the most exciting form of fishing imaginable. It is the best, almost the only way to make a bag of these shy fish when rivers are low. The best nights are those which follow warm days in settled weather conditions, coupled with as slight a drop in air temperature as possible. Very dark nights when the blackness is all-enveloping are not good. I prefer some moonlight diffused through cloud, or even clear starry nights. On any summer night but the blackest it should be possible to see the fall of the line across the river. Only one thing is fatal to sport at night: casting from a high position with the moon behind you.

Before night fishing a strange river you *must* go on a reconnaissance. Find out where the sea trout lie, the best places to stand and cast and the tricky places to be avoided. Move slowly and stick to one or two good pools. You can fish the same water several times over in a way that would be utterly hopeless by day. But remember, although the fish are not so wary by night they can still be frightened by sudden movements; a stumble wading along the shallows, or a splashy cast.

Casting a fly is no harder in the dark than during daylight, but any slight tangle caused by mistiming is trebly difficult to undo! Long casts which would be essential in daylight are *out* after dark. You don't need them when sea trout on the move obligingly come into the shallows. Trout tackle will serve admirably, but I tie slightly heavier casts *(a)* because sea trout run heavy and even the smaller ones can give a heavy snatch on a taut line, and *(b)* to keep the cast free of knots and tangles: fine nylon with sea-trout flies attached can snarl up.

Darkness doesn't seem to impair the ability of sea trout to see small flies on or under the surface. Never be afraid to fish small sizes and sober colours; this can be an advantage in the middle and upper reaches of rivers whose sea trout are becoming stale. Several spare casts should be carried with flies ready tied on. If the one being fished tangles or a fly is lost in a bush it is quicker to replace a whole cast. Use loop end casts with a knot on the end of your line. The knot joining cast and line is easily tied by feel.

Carry a torch in the fishing bag, but the less it is used the better. Never shine a light near the water you intend fishing for it will surely warn sea trout their public enemy number one is about! Even momentary use of a torch ruins your night vision for several minutes.

The other different item of equipment necessary in the dark is a large landing net with a stiff and easily visible rim. My net is a circular one with a silver ring which catches any light and would accommodate sea trout of twice the size I've yet caught. In the daytime, fish are often scooped up before they are played out; this is a dangerous habit in the dark. Beach fish where it is possible to do so without having to wade in and out of the water. If you have to net them, make sure they are tired and on their sides before sliding them into the meshes. Indeed, it's not easy to see exactly where they are until they show some flank or belly on top of the water. If you hook a large sea trout which you are most anxious to net safely, by all means use your torch. The fish will be worth the disturbance!

On most rivers you will find sea trout move best in the first hour of darkness. Many anglers, anxious not to miss too much sleep, pack up around midnight if they have not caught fish. By staying on another hour or more you may sometimes beat the experts and pick up a fish or two which did not move earlier.

Sea trout take in two places by night on the average river: on the shallows where they are moving around and sometimes feeding, or in their daytime positions where temperature or other conditions have induced them to stay. You need not worry about the second until the first possibility has failed. Most sea trout fishermen start fishing once it is *dark* towards the tail end of a good pool in which the fish are known to be lying—the theory being that taking fish generally drop back into the shallows and running fish often pause in the tail of a pool before going on up. Another good place to try is a shallow between two deeper areas of water. If shallow fishing fails you should fall back on the pools or deeper glides where the fish were resting during daylight. This calls for sunk line and, preferably, just one lure on the cast which will sink and bump their noses on its journey across the river.

With a hefty lure, fishing shallow water, unless it is very fast, merely means hitting bottom constantly and eventually getting snagged in a rock. So for the early part of the night on the shallows, stick to a fly (or preferably two flies) fished with a floating line close to the surface as described in the last section. As long as sea trout come up to the near-surface flies, stick to them and the floating line. After half-an-hour or so without a touch I switch to the deeper fishing. Much depends on the average depth and flow of the river. You can fish a bigger fly deeper in the Border Esk or lower Dovey than would be possible in Devon's Dart or Teign.

Every move made at night should be deliberate and without haste, and this applies most of all to working the fly. With the exception of a sedge imitation at dusk, I believe it will pay you to curb your impatience and work the fly slowly through the water. Let the current start its movement as it puts a slight belly in your line, and continue the movement of the fly with slow pulls on the line by hand. This applies to near-surface and deeply sunk flies. Movement, but steady movement, is the key to success.

As in reservoir casting, I'm not against varying the style of retrieve occasionally. A quick retrieve can be made every so often in the hope of changing a reluctant sea trout's mind. Like trout, they may follow a fly and slash at it just as it is lifted for the next cast. Most sea trout take as the flies swing across the current in that first deadly yard or two of movement. It pays to cast at least a yard further across river than you think the fish are lying in order to have the fly moving nicely and at the correct depth as it approaches them.

What is its correct depth? For surface-feeding fish your fly may be awash, or a few inches below the top of the water. For the dour residents which prefer to hang on to their daylight positions, it ought to sink to within a foot of the bottom, maybe six inches, to ensure it goes close enough to them.

Just as I believe in allowing the rod point to take the strain of a reservoir trout's take, so in sea trouting I would never point the rod tip down the line. Some fish take gently and must be struck by instinct as much as anything, but the normal take varies from a pluck or a steady draw to a hefty tug which—especially in the dark—seems to come from a veritable monster.

The moment a sizeable sea trout feels your well sharpened hook in his jaw he is off with a rush that cannot possibly be checked. Lift your rod well up and let him take all the line he wants. If he is hooked near the tail end of a pool and persists in going downstream, there's precious little you can do except slack off and hope he will turn back upstream at the last moment. If a big fish goes on down you must follow, or break!

There is, of course, no mistaking the rough, tough, savage pull of a good fish of 2lb and over. It takes time, however, to accustom yourself to the gentle takers which feel like small brown trout until you hit them. I make it a rule to lift my rod sharply when *anything* suspicious happens. Plenty of good fish have been hooked as a result which might otherwise have ejected the fly in time to save their skins. Successful fly fishing depends on your being one step ahead of them, all the time.

PRACTICE

It is early August, and we are on a lovely stretch of the Devonshire Teign. The weather is settled, the river low but by no means stagnant and we know there are plenty of peal of all sizes from school fish to near-monsters in this beat. There is a certain amount of cloud about and the moon is half way between new and full. On this stretch of association water, on the left bank above a weir, the moon won't be a bother until after midnight, as there is a well-wooded hill above the river to shield it. In fact, with cloud to diffuse its light and because you will be facing it, the moon will not worry you at all.

You know just what the river banks and river bed look like after some daytime exploration. I suggest you put up the 9ft rod and floating line with a two-fly cast tapering to 5lb b.s. for immediate use; I shall gillie for you and bring along the heavier rod with the sinking line and a level 7lb b.s. cast carrying one large lure.

Above the length you are going to fish there is a narrow rock gullet through which the river pours fiercely, and this steadies into a deep, black pool where there's a chance of a fish before true darkness. Trees shade it, and in such places you can begin fishing sooner without scaring the peal.

Wet your flies in the fast water just below the gullet, and, on your knees, fish them down and across the river where it steadies into the pool. Let the current swing the flies across and then draw them up a foot or so, very gently, before casting again. Yes, it's downstream sunk fly fishing again. A dozen casts in this spot will cover the area where peal may take. The river is very narrow indeed, no more than two rod lengths of fishable water I'd say. So for goodness sake don't hook the bushes or rocks on the opposite bank!

There you are! A splash at the tail fly, your No 10 Teal Blue and Silver, fishing shallow and fast; a thump on the rod tip and a pounder dancing a very hasty jig across the surface of the pool. Pity he didn't stay on, it would have been a good start to the night.

Almost dark now. We must be off to the quiet water, downstream towards the almost-dry weir. With luck, you will see or hear some peal jumping, or be able to see the hefty swirl of a feeding fish within reach.

Relax. Relax at all costs. This is one of the most exciting moments in sea-trout fishing: when the bats are flittering up and down the black, oily-looking surface of the river, when the first owl hoots and a big peal whirrs up and shatters the stillness of the evening with a walloping splash. You must avoid the temptation to get your flies out and start thrashing the water. Avoid hurry of any kind. Attune yourself to the darkness and the mood of the night. When it is calm and still, like this, and the river is reasonably low it is idiocy to begin fishing until it is absolutely dark. In fast water or in stormy conditions, begin at dusk by all means.

Sit down just back from the water's edge. Run your hand down the cast feeling for wind knots; ascertain that your dropper is hanging well, and clear of the cast; touch the hook points to be sure they are intact and *sharp*. Drop the flies in the water, and keep looking and listening for rises.

The stretch you will fish may give you a peal almost anywhere down its fifty or so even-flowing yards of water. There are two extra-likely places, however, which you saw in daylight. One is a depression in the river bed, a four-foot saucer with only a couple of feet of water upstream and downstream of it; and the other is a length under the alder bushes at the bottom end where you lay entranced watching a good shoal of peal up to 3lb.

In your gum boots—waders are not needed for this small river—you can step quietly down the bank, sometimes on rock sometimes just in the shallows, making no noise and casting as you go. The peal may come to you: or you may have to keep on the move after them. Whatever happens, you can fish a length like this optimistically several times a night, providing you do so carefully.

Start now, making short casts and keeping the flies nicely on the move without too much line disturbance. Drop them softly on the water, pausing several seconds to allow them *and* the cast to get under the surface film. Don't forget—fish slowly, do nothing in a hurry. Make a fairly acute angle between your rod tip and the line to cushion a shock take at short range. Lengthen line slightly with each cast until you have covered one sector of the river. Then move a pace or two downstream and start again. The illustration opposite shows what I mean.

On many rivers, and certainly this one, steady pace-at-a-time downstream fishing is impossible owing to bushes and other obstructions—hence the need to try and cover all the water from a staggered series of fishable places.

You felt something? Try the same cast again and fish it fractionally faster. Peal have a habit of gently nibbling at the fly—most frustrating! No good? Fish on down as if nothing had happened, there may be a hungrier fish below.

Another touch, and another! These peal certainly are choosy. Creep quietly upstream a few yards and rest the water for five

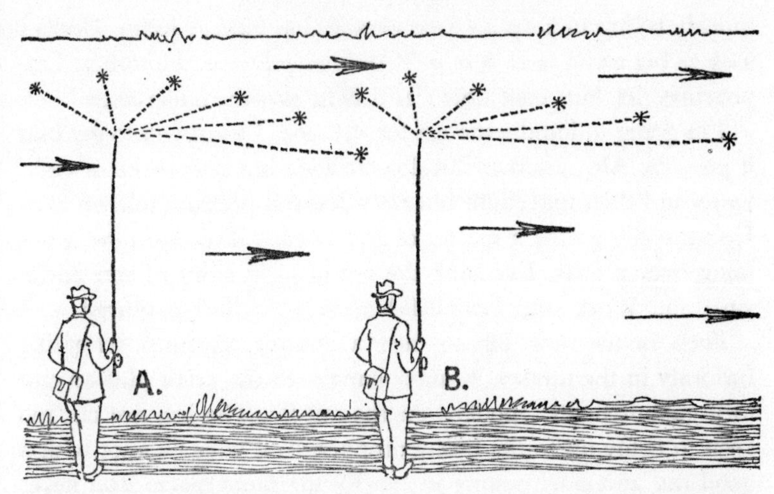

Sector casting: when you have tried (A) move down to (B) and repeat the process

minutes. Start casting again square across the stream to speed up the flies, and strike the *very* moment you suspect anything.

Got him! He jumped two feet in the air in hurt surprise. Since he's a school fish and not much above ½lb you can safely haul him upstream away from his mates.

One more hooked, though unfortunately lost, out of the next three touches. You might have done worse. The next gap in the bushes brings you within reach of the slightly deeper water and possibly a good fish or two. It's only 11 pm and the moonlight hasn't beamed over the hillside yet. Try this length very carefully. Make yourself *see* the fly as a sea trout does; a lithe little object moving through the water, steadily at first then in frenzied jerks —its body giving a gleam of silver in the gradually increasing glow from the moon. Think in terms of a good fish following your fly with interest *every* cast and fish it accordingly with close attention. You may get only one pull from a good fish in a night's casting but your steadfast care will be worth the effort if it's a three-pounder.

The shriek of your reel frightened me out of my night-time day dreaming! Let him go, and hold your rod high up, at shoulder height if need be to keep as much line as possible out of the water and away from snags. Now he's turned, and you must reel in quickly trying to keep an even pressure on him. A jump. Doesn't look as big as he feels does he? Another jump, and another. Less pressure; let him cool down and fight slower, underwater.

I'm going to handle the net for this one. I want you to get him if possible. Ah—another run downstream, but only seven or eight yards and then that slight but relentless rod pressure told on him. He's travelling only a matter of feet in each direction now, wobbling over a little. I've sunk the net dead in front of you and a yard out. Work your beaten fish in and . . . he's captured.

Feels better than 2lb to me: a chunky specimen wriggling furiously in the meshes. A quick bang with the priest puts an end to a gallant fighter, hooked on the tail fly. The fish are not too keen to come up to the bushy dropper. Test your fly knot with a good tug and start casting in exactly the same place. You never know! I'll retire into the meadow and put this fish on the spring balance by torchlight.

He's 2lb 5oz and looks so beautiful I'm convinced he's a 'she'. Hen trout, as they are called, are usually more shapely than the cock fish and very often their fight is livelier.

Nothing more? You've fished all the water once and it's still only 11.30 pm. Why not have a gulp of coffee and run down it again? Some of these school peal could have changed their minds by now....

They hadn't, and you are now feeling a lot less hot after the excitement of your monster (wait until you meet a six-pounder!) and wondering what to do next. Come with me, over the stile, and down to the deep flat just above the weir and its salmon steps. The moon is up now, coming and going behind light cloud, and I think you ought to try the deeply sunk lure and the sunk line. The fish are neither rising nor jumping so it's time you sent your fly down towards the river bed where they are lying.

The moonlight is illuminating this pool quite well. There are some handsome bushes growing along the banks at intervals, and nothing much else. Approach the water very carefully until you are in the shade of the first bush, upstream of it. Try casting out opposite the bush and fishing the fly slowly back to your own bank. The pool here is a good five feet deep and, if anything, a shade deeper under the bush itself. It's a good lie and might even hold a salmon, though it would be unusual if you hooked one at night.

With your sunk line you won't have to wait more than a few moments before starting to fish the fly in this slack water. It is going to drop on shallows of a couple of feet or less, and gradually work across the stream going deeper. Strike if you sense *any* interference with your tubc fly. Cast a little further downstream here to avoid any possibility of dragging a line across their noses before they see the lure.

I tied on a 1in Jungle Cock tube with a silver tinsel body and black streamer hair. It is attractive without being too gaudy. The treble hook size is 14, which is small but effective. A small treble usually gets a deep grip in the fish's mouth. Remember to vary the retrieve every so often with a series of quick pulls, or maybe a steady haul without any break in the fly's progress. Above all, get the fly well down, even bumping the river bed where it will interest, aggravate or infuriate the peal. Not so long ago, grubbing the bottom like this with the old Jungle Cock, I fairly hooked and landed a small eel. You never know what will happen out fishing.

You fished quite well round that bush, but nothing responded. If you can manage it, cast a few yards further, drawing off line a foot at a time and gradually working the fly downstream with each cast until you've reached your length limit. But to thrash about trying for an extra yard you can't manage, spoils the water for yourself and any other angler who may be following : better, then, to move yourself stealthily down the bank.

Let's go on down to the hedge. Opposite and below it there is another good bit of sea-trout water. Hear that one plunge? The first moving fish since midnight, and you could interest it.

Had a pull? You thought he was off, and then the rod was nearly pulled from your hand as you turned to tell me about it! That fish hooked himself as he took and immediately swam in towards you. It's impossible to keep in touch with those athletes except by stripping in line with your free hand faster than the reel could gather it. It's a bad practice, especially at night when you can't see what the loose line may be falling round (try disentangling it from a thistle in time to catch up with a peal travelling at speed) but it's the only way to keep a steady strain on the fish and consolidate the hook-hold.

Luckily this one is still on, giving you some anxious moments upstream under an overhanging bush. Hold your rod at arm's length as far out over the river as possible and persuade him to move out if you can. I was terrified he would snag you before you played him out. Now he's safe in the net, and I'd guess him around $1\frac{3}{4}$lb, which makes a very handsome brace to top the bag.

Time—around 2 am. An occasional good fish jumping. Let's try the remaining length above the weir before packing up. It will take between half an hour and an hour and there is a chance of a fresh-run peal from the lower reaches when you cast towards the top of the salmon steps. Those, by the way, are a series of stepped pools down one side of the weir face which take most of the flow of the river at normal and low level, enabling both salmon and peal to swim up.

Nothing more to the sunk line except a stone on the bottom which held the lure a moment and started your pulse jumping. You are almost at the end of the pool and it shallows off just above the weir so here's the lighter rod and floating line again—same flies. This will enable you to search all the holding water right to the lip of the weir.

There's rather more cloud over the moon now, a good sign. And that little fish took you with a rush and a splash. A very small school peal of probably less than $\frac{1}{2}$lb. They have a way of leaping vertically when hooked, very different from most brown trout.

He's off. Never mind, you caught the largest of the evening so it was no hardship to lose the smallest. It's been a grand night and I'm sure you'll want to fish plenty more like it. You will certainly have some better nights, in terms of both numbers and size of fish, and I can guarantee you many when you won't do anything like so well.

CHAPTER ELEVEN

SALMON: *Spring Fishing—Sunk Line*

THEORY

FIRST, a few words about salmon. They are the largest fish you are likely to kill on fly in this country. Cynics may consider them cheaper to buy on fishmongers' slabs than they are to fish for, and the cynics are often right!

Salmon are not as dashing as sea trout but they do run larger. Their taking times are still less predictable. But the take of a salmon on a fly rod is exciting, and it may come at any time even on a hot summer day. No creeping about in the darkness for these fish!

Different rivers offer different runs of salmon. The season normally opens between January and March, which is spring in the salmon angler's calendar, but on some rivers you may have to wait until May or June for the fish, or even for the spates of August and September. In certain rivers, mainly in the north, there are autumn runs of fish which can be sought until November. Your season can be a lengthy one taking you to many rivers —if you can afford it. The more you spend on salmon fishing the more fish you are likely to recoup: but rewards are not automatic. Most of us have to be content with a rented share in a fishery, membership of an association or holidays on hotel waters.

It pays to learn a river thoroughly when fishing for its salmon. If you have but a short time in which to fish a strange water, employ a gillie or accept as much local advice as possible on the lies of the salmon. Salmon are moody fish and may ignore lures for long periods under apparently ideal conditions. All of a sudden they start taking—if you are still on the river and trying! They do, however, run into the same pools on their rivers year after year and lie in the same places; this is where local knowledge comes in, especially on the cold days of spring when the fish decline to 'show' on the surface.

Many good salmon are killed on trout rods every season, and that great Wye angler, Robert Pashley, caught many of his thousands of salmon on such light tackle, fish of up to 40lb too. But it is asking too much of a trout rod to fling a size 1/0 salmon fly across a broad river in spring, or to lift a heavy sunk line. For this reason, primarily, you must acquire something sturdier than your heavier reservoir trout rod.

The length of your salmon-fly rod will vary according to the rivers you are likely to fish. The Wye or some of the big rivers of Scotland in early spring and late autumn when sunk line and fly are used demand rods of 13ft to 15ft built for hard work. The smaller your river, and the smaller your fly, the nearer you are to a light trout rod again. It all depends on the fly, not the weight of the fish you expect to encounter. I have:

A 12ft built cane rod	£15
4in fly reel	£5
30 yards, GAG line spliced to 100 yards of backing	£6 10s
Flies (not too many patterns, but in most sizes 1/0 to 10)	5s each approx.
And a landing implement (net, tailer or gaff)	£5

The costs are approximate. I haven't added in nylon because it is very cheap and you will already have some suitable strengths in your tackle bag. Don't go below 10lb b.s. until you've tested your tackle against a good few fish. In spring I would not fish finer than 12lb b.s. and some anglers consider that 'cobweb' strength!

What else you put in your tackle bag rather depends on you. A thermometer to show water temperatures is useful; so is a spring balance to register the truthful weight of your catch; and you will need a spare reel with a floating line on it—I use my reservoir reel and line. Carrying any salmon is no joke after the first few hundred yards, so have a commodious tackle bag, keep a bass handy or make a rope-and-hook carrier which will hold the fish by its gills and tail (see illustration opposite).

Flies for salmon come in all sorts of patterns and types. I take

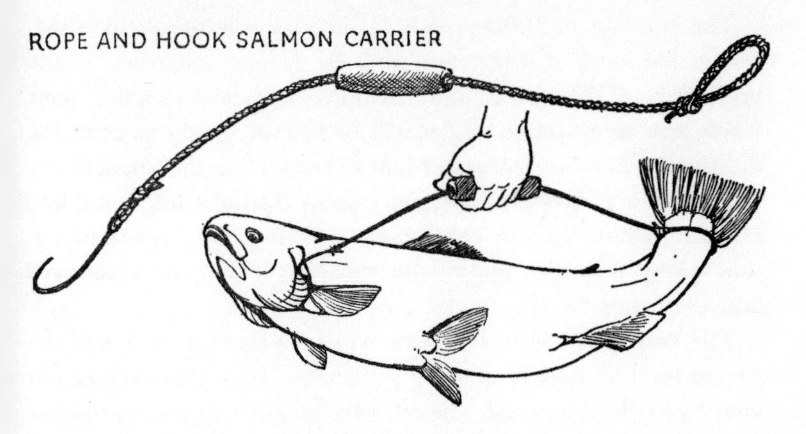

an interest in patterns only in a general way, choosing bright or dull colour combinations according to conditions. Types vary a good deal, from the traditional single hook to the treble-hook tube or Waddington variety : you can get double-hook flies and singles with a joint in the middle of the body too.

I favour Silver Grey, a bright fly; Thunder and Lightning, neither bright nor sombre; Blue Charm, similar to the Thunder and an attractive floating line pattern when the fish want the lure close to the surface; and a Stoat's Tail or something similar with black hair which looks like a big juicy nymph. Never hesitate to add any recommended local killer to the list on a strange river. Sizes should vary from 1/0 down to a 10 (salmon scale). Anything larger than 1/0 is too big for rods of 12ft or less and probably no more effective than the smaller fly; anything smaller than a No 10 is not likely to hold well in the jaw of a big fish, or indeed to hook it at all.

As a general rule, choose a bright, showy fly with some yellow or orange in its make-up for coloured water, gradually toning down patterns as the river becomes clearer. I haven't yet decided whether it's better to fish a very bright or very dull fly in normal sunshine conditions. Much depends on how fresh the salmon are from the sea. If I was forced to select either showy or drab flies, and given no latitude, I should go for the drab ones—while strongly missing that touch of flashiness from a jungle cock feather or a tinsel body !

The method of fishing your fly in spring is simplicity itself. Remember your downstream sunk fly fishing for trout at the beginning of the season and you have it almost exactly. Your whole aim as a salmon angler will be to slow up the pace of the fly through fast running water and to keep it moving attractively, but slowly and deep, in the quieter pools. Spring salmon and late autumn salmon run in cold water and they are slow-thinking, slow-taking fish. The longer you can hold a fly over a salmon's nose the better.

The best fished lure is the one which swings gently across the stream level or slightly above your salmon. Nine times out of ten your lure will be ignored: the odds are usually still greater against you. Then the magic moment arrives and *your* fish will turn and suck in the fly, or slash up at it with a dramatic twist of its body, grabbing it and giving a breathtaking pull as it turns back towards its lie. This tremendous pull is what makes salmon fishing in the cold months so exciting.

The longer your cast and the further downstream you fish it the better it will show the fly to the salmon. Until April, even on warm, southern rivers, it may be best to depend on the sunk fly; from then until September the near-surface fly comes into its own with water temperatures of 10 degrees Centigrade (around 50 degrees Fahrenheit). There is a world of inquiry left open for scientific minds as to why salmon want a large, sunk fly in low water temperatures (and sometimes when air temperatures drop sharply) and a fly almost awash when rivers warm up.

How you fish your fly depends on the type of water at your disposal. On a small river whose current, for example, runs between midstream and the far bank, you can expect the fish to lie in that sector. You would probably reach it without wading. On such rivers I do not expect early salmon to move very far or fast in pursuit of a lure, so having allowed the fly to move gently across the best area of a pool it can be hauled out and cast a yard further downstream for the next try. On a large river whose fish are well spread out you should fish your fly back across the stream until it is almost below you, and even then do not hurry to lift it from the water for the next cast.

Always, always keep a foot or more of free, slack line hanging

Into him! An Exe salmon is hooked and the angler has left the water and wisely stationed himself well up the bank, keeping most of his heavy fly line out of the river too

Which fly today? Time of year, air and water temperature play a part in our choice

close to the reel. If a determined fish grabs your fly on a taut line and you hit him too quickly you may lose him. Salmon, unlike trout, like to hang on to a lure until they are back in their lies. Stale fish may not always do so, but fresh-run salmon are generally as slow to release a lure as they are to take it.

The take will vary from a sudden throbbing pull, whipping up all your slack line and bending the rod over almost instantaneously, to a slow, suspicious draw with a second or two elapsing before you realise a fish is responsible. Try and react calmly; be as slow as the salmon in making up your mind to pull the hook home. A good rule is *never* to pull at the fish before he has pulled your rod point decisively. A well-hooked salmon can be played hard from almost any angle without danger of loss. Lightly hooked fish will sooner or later come adrift. For the sake of your sport *and* the fish, it is better to lose one quickly and go in search of another.

One of the few undeniable features of salmon angling is the way in which they come on the take together. Sometimes killing one in a certain place is a really good indication that you will take another! Almost always the fish will be hooked below you, and you may wonder how the hook-hold comes to be pulled into its jaws as if from downstream. The answer is in your sunk, *slack* line which imposes the necessary strain to drive the hook home after the fish has turned back towards its lie. The water pressure on your line bellying round does almost as much to hook the fish as your steady lifting of the rod.

Never relax pressure unless the fish heads towards danger in the shape of a snag or the rapids into the pool below. Try and keep as much of the line as you can out of the water; too much heavy line out in a strong current exerts great pressure on the hook-hold. The way to tire a salmon is to draw him sideways, upsetting his balance against the current. Unsettle him if he 'sits down' and sulks. Keep your rod well up, but don't hesitate to swing it horizontally, close to the river surface, and get a sideways pull on the fish when necessary.

I never like salmon running directly up or downstream of me, preferring to conduct the fight almost opposite them. I don't believe it much matters if you stay above or below the fish as long as you keep worrying them. If you want to work a fish upstream to a suitable landing place, or stop him from rushing downstream, hold the rod close to the water, leave your reel handle alone and start walking slowly. Usually the fish follows—the movement doesn't greatly inconvenience him.

If you are accompanied by an experienced hand, your hooked fish may be landed before it is fully played out, especially if a gaff is used. Otherwise, ensure the fish *is* beaten before you attempt to make him yours. There's a world of difference between a quarter-pound trout sliding into a net and a 10lb salmon coming to hand.

I prefer to beach salmon where this is possible, walking slowly back across the shingle or rock and working the fish quietly inshore until their heads are well out of the water. It is achieved most safely on a long line—which helps to keep you and your shadow out of sight of the fish. They lie quietly when the strain is relaxed. Lay down your rod, reel handle uppermost, and walk behind the fish to grasp its tail and *push* it completely ashore before lifting it up and carrying it a few yards from the water. Don't walk on the rod in your excitement!

Salmon can be tailed by hand while still in the water. Get a vicious thumb-and-first-finger grip on their tail end just above the fin; your whole hand is more hindrance than help. Very occasionally a grip in the gills is easier—if you have almost killed a fish in deep water close to the bank his head may pop up while his tail flops to the bottom. A mechanical tailer is useful, but they can slip off a fish. Once I ran one so far up a salmon his head slipped through the wire noose and I tailed the line! I played him and the tailer back and got him with a gill grip. Nets are best left to gillies or friends: they are far too large and cumbersome for solitary anglers.

Gaffs are disliked in certain quarters owing to the wound they leave in a fish. But this needn't be a large one, and I know of no safer and certainly no quicker method of landing a large fish. Once a fish ceases struggling and comes within reach of the gaff it is not difficult to draw the sharp hook into its back or belly and, with an unhurried, smooth movement, lift it to the bank. Aim for the middle of the fish so that it balances well on the gaff. They rarely struggle unless you jerk about and upset the smooth movement. Don't slash at a fish with the gaff, of course, for if you scrape it the fight will start again; and be sure your cast is well clear of your gaff point. There is an art in gaffing, as in all things. I've had a large gaff point badly twisted by a struggling seven-pounder, and safely hauled a salmon more than twice that weight up a five-foot bank with the aid of a tiny trout gaff (which I never use for trout).

Do not—as I've actually witnessed on the banks of the Exe—give your salmon one light tap on the head and then stand back to admire it at the water's edge. That 10lb fish jumped convulsively and regained its freedom with nothing worse than a sore cranium! Carry your fish well away from the river and give him three or four hearty raps with the priest—quickly.

Finally, a word of warning about kelts, which are salmon on their downstream journey to the sea after spawning. It is illegal to kill them, morally wrong but all to frequently done by beginners. Most of the kelts which return to the sea will not survive to make a second spawning trip, but this is no justification for slaying them. They are not good food and many of them look emaciated and ugly.

The problem fish are the ones which ran late into the river, spawned almost immediately and did not lose very much weight or their good looks; and there are the so-called 'well mended' kelts which have turned silvery and fight with some vigour. On the Exe, my principal salmon fishing of the moment, kelts are easily detected. They look positively snaky and their heads are enormous against their thin bodies. Overleaf are illustrations of a kelt compared with a fresh salmon.

Fresh-run springers have a blue-brown back and a creamy look about their flanks as they turn in the water. Mended kelts are a metallic blue on top and very silvery on the flanks. If you are pretty sure the fish you have hooked is a kelt—and in some pools early in the season, if there is low water, the odds are on this happening—pull it in, handling it very firmly. Hold it down gently with one hand, extract the fly and slip the fish back over the shallows, making sure it has enough strength to swim off. Don't be guilty of returning a salmon, or any other fish, which is bleeding

badly or floating belly up. Nurse them in a moderate current, holding them upright if necessary until they recover.

Kelts often have ragged lower fins, and normally their vents are still distended. Their gills are ragged too and may be covered with parasites known as gill maggots. Once you have compared a fresh salmon and a kelt on the river bank you are not likely to make many future mistakes. If you are ever in doubt, return the fish, you've had your fun.

And now to make a start on salmon fishing, let's be off to that stretch of the Exe you first whipped with your sunk flies downstream. We'll be trying it on 1 March, a fortnight after the season's opening day.

PRACTICE

Here's the familiar farmyard. It's good to be back after the winter lay-off. The last time I threw a fly for salmon was miles further up the Exe in September: and a lively twelve-pounder obliged.

Conditions today are very different. The water temperature is around 5 degrees Centigrade (40 degrees Fahrenheit) and air temperature very little warmer. The river was high at the beginning of the season; not enough to bring many fish through from the sea but sufficient to encourage some of the earliest arrivals to work their way over the weirs from lower beats. Spring salmon have been caught several miles above here in the past fortnight, so there's a chance. I shall be surprised if you don't have one or two false alarms from kelts.

It was frosty this morning and there's a distinctly chilly edge to the breeze blowing down the valley. Put up the 12ft rod and attach the reel with the sinking line. A 6ft cast will do, 12lb b.s. blood-knotted to the yard of 16lb nylon linked with the line.

There's no colour in the water; it has that attractive greenish tinge which cold, dry weather brings, so try a size 1 single hook Thunder and Lightning for a start. By the way, most salmon flies are tied on an up-eyed hook and need a knot different from the one you've been using up to now. Use the Double Turle knot, it goes like this:

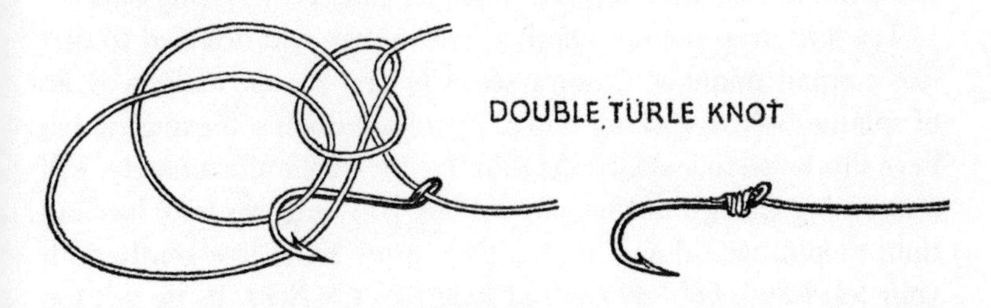

Your starting point is towards the tail of this pool. There's more than six feet of water under the bushes which spread out from our bank, the right bank, and some large stones around which the salmon lie. Don't let the fly fish too deeply for fear of hitching up on that underwater stone rampart. If it gets down between four and five feet there will be a chance—I don't believe salmon lie with their bellies actually touching the bed of the river.

The bank is rather high on your side, but happily it is not quite vertical so you slide down the soft soil closer to the water. It's too deep to wade. The current in this pool is sufficiently strong to swing your fly across at just the right speed if you aim it well downstream. Most of the fish lie in the deepest section of the pool between midstream and your bank. The stones, which set up a very slight swirl on the surface, are about thirty yards from the tail of the pool and your chance of a pull may be anywhere from ten yards upstream of them to twenty yards below, where the river begins to shallow.

Casting a sizeable fly with a heavy sunk line is easy if you don't hurry. You will, of course, use both hands on the 12ft rod, your left hand being close to the reel, where it will be needed to take care of the slack line as the fly fishes round. Twenty yards of line out will be plenty to cover this pool. The drill is to lift steadily at the end of a cast until most of that line is out of the water or on its way upwards and then, with an acceleration of the rod tip, get the whole lot cleanly up in the air and straightened out behind you. No false casting! Try and do it in one motion as smoothly as possible and *do* take a long pace down the bank between every cast or you will never cover all the available water. It is much, much better when fishing for salmon to cover a pool twice in an hour than to plod down it painstakingly only once.

Try and drop the fly quietly, even though it is destined to sink like a small minnow. I don't see why you should make a series of splashes when working down a pool although some anglers believe this helps to liven up the salmon; the line, unfortunately, will make a big enough disturbance. When you judge your fly has had time to sink well down after a cast, draw some line gently with your left hand, holding the rod steady in the right, its tip not too far from the water. This ensures the fly starts to fish on an even keel.

Now the current takes over on the slight belly in the line and draws it round, its hair or hackles quivering in the water making it look alive and attractive. When it has plainly come across the river and started to hang downstream of the extended rod point, start a gentle retrieve just in case a fish has followed in and still wants it. The upstream movement may make it grab. I don't think you need move the rod tip before the fly has swung across, though some people like to add motion to it by waggling the rod tip from side to side or lifting and dropping it alternately.

If you do want to hurry the fly across the pool and keep it moving quite fast right into your own bank, point the rod not towards the water but down the bank and slightly inland, and extend it further inland stripping in line too as you near the end of the fly's travel. This is a likely cast over a fish which has just moved if you can get the fly into the area quickly enough.

I use the expression 'moved' as opposed to 'jumped' because salmon which actually leave the water entirely, flopping back heavily, are rarely taking fish. The hopeful ones in spring are those which perform a quiet head-and-tail rise, or, better still, swirl up with a hefty slap of their tail on the surface.

You have now fished beyond the best point of this pool in normal water conditions. When a small flood is running it can fish well towards the tail end, but not now. Settled spring salmon like a moderate depth and current: they always avoid extremes.

I see your rod bent into a half-hoop, and presume the fly has snagged itself on something in the shallows. Walk downstream of it and lift the line as high out of the water as possible, giving it a rippling shake as you do so. Still tight? Go back where you were and pull off yards more line—yards and yards. Then cast all the spare line, in the usual way, towards and beyond the snagged fly. The sudden pull of the line from an opposite direction should clear it.

Sorry you had no excitement in the first pool but it's not the best of fly water, being too deep and steady altogether. Places where you see surface current rippling the water and bringing it to life are the ones to head for with a fly rod—providing there is also a reasonable depth with lies for the fish.

Let's walk downstream past the run where you got your first trout last year to a swifter and narrower pool whose water boils along beside a number of stones used to protect and support the opposite bank. In low water the head of this pool is a delectable place for the fly. At present it is far too high and rapid, so you must start thirty or forty yards further down. Even then it will be necessary to wade thigh deep and hold the rod tip well across the stream to try and slow down the fly's progress.

On the far bank of this pool there are a number of willow bushes, good cover for salmon, and an excellent spot for a pull is opposite the old gatepost below them. It's all good holding water as far as you can see until the river vanishes in a right-hand bend behind a high shingle bank. I'm going to fish behind you down this pool so be sure to keep on the move, taking a long step between each cast. Normally I move forward at the split second my fly hits the water: it saves disturbing the rhythm of the lift-and-cast motion and gives the fly slack line to help sink it.

No, I'm not at all bothered about your fishing first down the pool. Salmon don't necessarily favour first-comers. We might cover this water twice each and still have our eyes wiped by some late arrival on his first try down!

Let me see more slack line hanging below your reel.

Now what? The rod top is bending and jerking and you are holding on grimly. I suspect you've hooked one of the numerous kelts. You had an unmistakable pull and merely lifted the rod slowly against it. Now keep the rod well up, and come steadily out of the river without losing touch with the fish.

Whatever it is has decided to play a sullen game of head shaking in midstream. Apply more lateral pressure and make him fight harder. Don't fiddle too much with the reel handle; instead, hold your line lightly against the rod and walk him towards the shallows. This should make the fish fight its way out again. There's no reason here why you shouldn't pull him downstream as there's a couple of hundred yards of easy flowing pool below you and no hazards.

Sorry! He really looks like a kelt. The absence of any thrusting upstream runs is a fair indication, and a true spring fish wouldn't give up so quickly. Walk inland, firmly, and *make* the fish follow. I can assist him ashore gently and show you what's wrong with him.

Would you kill a trout looking as thin and scruffy as that? I've unhooked the fly—it had a nice deep grip in the corner of his jaw—and you shall return him. Grip his tail end firmly, support him with the other hand under his body and gently send him upstream into the pool. A lively fellow that. Two flicks of his tail and he was away. I hope he (more likely she) will return a second time to the river. Many a clean fish wouldn't have fought much better than your kelt, if that's any consolation!

No more thrills, and it's lunchtime. We can eat our sandwiches opposite the next pool, an awkward corner where the river twists in an 'S' round a large willow. We might see a fish move there.

Good of the sun to gleam through. The day has turned benign and I reckon there's an excellent chance of a fish this afternoon.

Nothing moved here, but I know where the fish should be: in the fast stretch of water beyond that sunken tree surrounded with all the debris from the winter floods. Between the dead tree and the living willow downstream is 'fly' water. Below the willow I defy anyone to cast a fly nicely because of the mass of branches overhead. It can be flicked out and hung in the current, but the current is very strong even in low water; altogether it's a difficult place.

You will have to wade the river to the left bank in order to cover that run beyond the sunken tree. Go in about ten yards upstream of the point you want to reach on the far side and wade steadily across and downstream. Move each foot deliberately, and be sure they 'anchor' firmly in turn. Don't let the current hurry you. This water is fished from the bank which is about three feet above the river surface. It is a short cast and I suggest you try it standing well back from the edge so that only your rod top protrudes. It's foolish to frighten salmon unnecessarily.

You're doing nicely. About a dozen more casts and you will be swinging the fly as close as you dare to the old leaning willow. Further you cannot go—or cast.

What a shriek from the reel! The fish went downstream after taking, but almost immediately turned back upstream and could well be a real springer. He's full of spirit. Reel in like mad and keep in touch! Don't let him pull the rod point down horizontally like that again or he may break away. Try and keep him up towards the head of the pool. If he rushes down it will be very difficult to follow through the bankside 'jungle' by the willow, and it's impossible to wade. Ease the pressure when he goes away downstream. He will then turn to face up again and you should be able to draw him forward and regain the lost yards of line.

Nearly ten minutes mixed joy and anguish for you. He is tiring now, his creamy flanks are showing beneath the fast flowing stream. Try and hold him under your rod tip and start lifting and turning him in small circles if he tries to run. There can't be much finesse playing a salmon in an awkward place like this.

See how he rolled belly up for a moment? But he recovered

and made another strong dive for the bottom. If you can walk up just a couple of yards and 'pump' him with a strong lift of the rod, I may be able to slip the tailer loop over him. We aren't allowed to use a gaff this early in the season because of the kelts.

Steady—another foot if you can manage it slowly without scaring him. I daren't move until he's within easy reach. Nothing is worse than making a bosh shot in such a place. If he was frightened enough to make a dash below the willow you'd have a dickens of a job working him back up—he would be too tired to help you by swimming up. Keep that gentle pressure on, I think I can reach. . . . Got him!

Firmly tailed, kicking with the shock of leaving the river so rudely, but held solid by the cable wire loop. Back we go, yards from the river, and my statutory number of whacks with the priest have killed your first salmon—a handsome eight-pounder with that faint tinge of pink along his sides denoting a springer which has been in the river some weeks. Is there a finer sight after hours of casting and the thrill, but worried thrill of the fight? Now you can relax with pride, mop your sweating brow, and collapse on the grass alongside the fish, *your* fish.

Between us and the farmyard there is another possible place for a salmon—the tail end of the second pool you tried where it flows gently into a wider reach of the river. Just before it widens is the spot, between two of the well-pruned willow bushes. When you've emptied the tea flask and torn your admiring gaze away from the fish we'll move there. *You* carry the fish.

Between those bushes in your best chance, so start about fifteen yards upstream of the first and work the fly down to it. It's smooth flowing water and the deepest part is very close to the far bank, which means wading and dropping your fly as close to that bank as you can. By the time you have fished it down once it will be nearly dusk—when I believe salmon liven up and sometimes actually start running even in moderately low water. Dusk is a very promising time for salmon, even on the coldest days.

It has gone colder now and normally this and failing light would indicate the need for a larger fly; but you are trying smooth and rather shallow water and your fly must be close to the river bed most of the time so it will do. Whether you fish on and on into the darkness depends on you. Once I had a February thirteen-pounder here which wasn't beached until it *was* dark; I always finish casting for salmon, however, at the moment I should regard as the earliest starting time for sea trout.

Nothing doing? I'm sorry my pet spot was disappointing, but if you had caught another salmon I'd have made you carry both of them back to the farmyard!

CHAPTER TWELVE

SALMON: *Summer Fishing—Greased Line*

THEORY

ONE of the most attractive features of salmon fishing is the way fish will come up to the surface to take a small fly from late spring onwards when water temperatures approach 10 degrees Centigrade (50 degrees Fahrenheit). Unless air temperature is immoderately colder, this habit is invariable and a source of joy to those who like using lighter tackle and seeing some of their fish take.

Known as greased-line fishing, for the simple reason that when it came in earlier this century fly fishermen used silk lines and had to grease them to keep them afloat, the method might more accurately be called floating-line fishing. Even this is a slight misnomer because many modern floater lines are actually designed to fish *just* under the surface (which can be an advantage) and some people like to tackle salmon with light trout lines, also awash, saying these frighten fish less than heavy lines floating on the surface. Both, unfortunately, cast shadows on the bright days when small, greased-line flies do well. Fish as light as you dare to obtain the most sport.

The whole art of the greased-line method lies in presenting a fly close to the surface film of the river, but not floating on it. British salmon rarely take any fly sitting on top of the water.

Size of fly has a distinct bearing on one's sport, and the most popular grease-line starting size is a No 6. In very low water with stale fish to contend with you may eventually reduce to a No 10 —or startle the pundits by raking out one of the veterans of the pool on a size 1/0. Rules in fishing are, of course, always made to be broken!

Your tackle for this fishing is the same: except for a reel containing floating line and a cast tapered down to 10lb b.s. instead of 12lb b.s., or perhaps 7lb b.s. if conditions warrant it. Later you may prefer to use a trout rod and still lighter cast. Your flies will be dressed sparsely on lighter hooks than the early spring variety. They are designed to swim shallow instead of sinking. Many of them will be dressed only half way along the hook shanks. No matter how tiny a morsel your fly may seem, salmon will spot it and come for it if the mood takes them.

Sunk flies more or less fish themselves; the greased-line method calls for some work on your part, which makes it all the more interesting. If you are fishing a genuine floating line you will be able to control the speed your fly travels across the river by 'mending' the line, as illustrated in the sea trout section. Use this in fast currents to slow down the fly's progress.

When casting far across a wide, rough stream this 'mending' may be necessary several times to keep down the pace of the fly as it swings over the salmon lies. Even in warmer, shallow water salmon will be slow to make up their minds, though they may sometimes chase a fly for yards in a manner most unlike their early spring behaviour.

Doubtless you've realised by now some belly in the line can also be an ally, not an enemy to be 'mended'. On a slow-running pool with no obvious surface current, you should cast across rather than downstream and so ensure a healthy belly does form in your line to pull the fly across at a reasonable speed. Pulling flies by hand is best not attempted with a floating line; it creates a wake on the surface which may disturb the salmon in quiet water. Do it, by all means, if you use a light trout line just sunk. At all times ensure your cast is under the water surface—that is most important.

Providing your fly doesn't sink more than a few inches it is behaving correctly. The closer it is to the surface the more likely you are to see a salmon take it, or create a lovely swirl in the water when it comes up and changes its mind at the last moment. Don't hurry to strike unless you have missed a fish or two and believe they are rejecting the fly unusually quickly. I like to feel the line drawing down the rod tip and then hook the fish. Always, if you move a salmon and miss it—or it misses you—try again with the same fly after a minute's pause. If nothing happens, try a smaller fly of the same pattern. Change fly sizes rather than patterns when greased lining, but don't neglect a change of type—from light body to very dark, for instance, or single hook to a small double or tube fly.

There is no reason why you should not fish a pair of flies on the cast. I like to offer salmon a dropper about four feet away from the tail fly but it probably matters little if they are closer. Two chances are better than one, and the fish can be offered a choice of patterns and sizes, each fly behaving slightly differently in the water. The risk of one fly becoming snagged while playing a salmon is worth taking for the additional advantage it gives.

In late spring when the greased-line method comes in, salmon are generally found in the expected lies, tucked just out of the main current in water of reasonable depth. Usually there are fish at the very head of each pool, where the water runs swiftly, and your lure must be slowed down and held over their noses. But there will be more fish further down the pools where the current is less noticeable. There will be precious few, however, in the rapids leading into a pool, or the long, shallow tail end. Reserve the latter for high-water fishing when salmon are on the move, and visit the rapids, the white water bursting its way through the rocks, early on summer mornings or last thing at night when low-water conditions prevail.

Fishing very fast water is easier than it looks—but it is fairly shallow, of course, so keep out of sight! Where a river narrows, it is usually at its fastest. It may be so narrow that instead of fishing your fly across the current you will have to drop it in below the rod point and let it downstream a foot at a time. Always keep the rod point well up and have plenty of slack line available. Don't be shy of quite unlikely-looking rushes of current in very hot weather. Salmon like a refresher, indeed the oxygen in such water is essential to them.

Keep your flies up towards the surface as long as conditions demand it—normally such conditions continue into September. When the first frosts begin to whiten the riverside meadows you can start fishing the sunk fly again.

If you are lucky enough to fish a river with a good grilse run your greased-line fishing will be greatly prolonged. Grilse are small salmon which return to the river after a year and a few months in the sea instead of the two years plus of normal salmon. They average around 6lb and are lively fighters, though sometimes difficult to tempt.

To my mind, May and September are the months for the greased line (in the south anyway) and May is the best because the salmon are invariably fresher from the sea, and not so far from it. But we have fished one spring day already so, for a practical demonstration of the floating line, come north with me in September to the Nith in Dumfriesshire—where I caught my first salmon on fly.

PRACTICE

It was a grilse—my first salmon—and it weighed 6lb. It took a small Haslam, the Welsh sea-trout fly, and I blush to admit it was almost twenty-five minutes before I lifted the fish up the bank on my little trout gaff, having crossed the river waist deep in thigh waders and then re-crossed it, dropping downstream to the next pool in the process.

The stretch of the Nith I've brought you to is association-controlled and a fair distance from the sea. That doesn't matter much because four days ago there was a splendid spate which brought up plenty of grilse, some summer salmon and a sprinkling of sea trout. Every pool on the several miles of river at our disposal holds salmon. Today the river looks delightfully clear and already a couple of anglers are hard at it, one worming the quicker water above the bridge and his pal spinning the slow depths below it.

It is misty and decidedly cool at this time of the morning, but we can be confident of a warm, sunny day once the sun does beam through. That, incidentally, is one of the likeliest moments with the fly. All the locals say so and you'll hear it said whatever river you fish.

This isn't a particularly wide river. It can be covered without wading in most places, and there are plenty of attractive, open pools for the fly. Some of the best stands are on knife-edge rocks, so watch your footing.

We can set up our tackle on the bridge and watch the worm fisherman at work. Nothing static about his methods, you'll notice. The bunch of lobs is kept on the move down a likely run and then lifted out and dropped in at the top again. He's in touch with his bait all the time, ready for the shy plucking of a salmon. You will try it some time, I expect, and marvel how easy fly fishing is by comparison.

As this outing is a joint affair we are going to set up the 12ft rod, sunk line and medium size fly, a No 4 Silver Grey will do, for use while the cool mist is still on the water and, possibly, at the end of the day when it strikes cool again; and the floating line and two-fly cast on the 9ft rod. Let's put up a No 8 Stoat's Tail on the dropper and a No 6 Blue Charm or Silver Blue for the tail fly. Some of the best casts here are narrow runs of water through rock, and none of the pools are enormous, so tie on the flies 2ft 6in apart.

Let's walk down the left bank a few hundred yards and try a small pool formed where the river winds into a sharp left bend. The head of the pool holds at least one salmon, I saw it move yesterday, and it's not an easy place for the association wormers as the opposite bank is rough going.

This is a place where accuracy counts. You must drop your fly inches from the far bank, if possible at the very head of the pool. It is about two feet deep at the head, but there is an underwater ledge with a drop of a further two feet and that is where the first salmon lies. If your fly drops accurately it will just miss the ledge and show for a moment in front of the fish. It's a matter of seconds only before the cast is completed and you must repeat it a foot or so downstream. A dozen casts and you are finished with the most likely taking place, though the middle of the pool does produce an occasional salmon.

Take the bigger rod and wade a yard or two out on the shallows at least fifteen yards upstream of your target. Make the fly travel slowly by holding the rod tip well out across the river, pointing in the direction of the salmon lie. Keep it up and let the line hang down slackly, with a foot of slack in your free hand.

No good. You fished it rather hastily first time down and tended

Gaffed! An Oykel salmon comes ashore

A satisfactory ending—an 8 lb salmon on the bank

to slam the fly into the same 'bull's eye' two or three times and then miss a couple of yards of water.

On we go to the next pool, and from the silver gleam through the mist I suspect we shall be nicely in time to try it with greased-line tackle. Let's hope a salmon will be on the look-out as the sun comes through. It is now eleven o'clock.

This is a typical salmon pool. The river gushes through rock and several large boulders with a powerful midstream current. This gradually widens out and grows calmer: the surface is smooth but there are signs here and there of submerged rocks which create good salmon lies. And at the tail end the river narrows again and runs smoothly and quite deep to a miniature fall. The widest part of this pool can be covered easily with the 9ft rod, and there are no obstructions at the rear to complicate casting.

Give the flies and cast a good bath in the shallows, and lengthen your line to start fishing down towards the two great boulders at the head of the pool. I doubt if the water is more than three feet deep between the boulders; it is very fast and should be fished by hanging the flies in it as long as possible.

That's the style. Don't wade too deep, you will have to come out to get round the boulder on this side and there's no need to wade beyond it. In fact, now you've tried the head of the pool and drawn blank I suggest you step two or three paces back from the edge of the river and fish the nearer water first. You will leave the salmon beyond midstream undisturbed for a second try down the pool when the sun is properly through.

Cast well downstream here where the current is swift enough to pull your flies round; as you progress twenty or thirty yards down the pool it will pay you to cast squarer across to achieve the necessary line belly and tension on the flies. Down there you will not be able to fish the dropper a'dangle as it was in the fast water; instead it will be swimming round like the tail fly.

Nothing, nothing at all, in fifty yards of good water with the sight of a moving fish upstream in a place the flies must have covered. Oh yes, it's typical salmon fishing. You must keep quietly on, without fluster, patiently awaiting *the moment*.

Now for the tail of the pool, and the last few yards may well hold a fish, for it is not shallow water and there are good resting places for salmon. Here you must wade, and hold the flies in the current.

Nothing? But you haven't quite finished your job because the last cast swung round at least three yards above the tail end of the pool. You could make a couple more casts, I'm sure, and you never know—there might be a stray sea trout waiting for the lure.

Right. It was a blank. No one else has appeared so you may as well fish down the pool again, reaching further across this time to cover all the water. What? You felt a tug and the rod bent heavily for a moment? It could have been a salmon. Maybe you had insufficient slack line to allow him to turn with the fly. Your rod tip has been rather too close to the water for much of the time.

Go back upstream several yards, take a quick look at both hook points and *don't* touch the reel. Strip line in by hand, then you'll be casting out exactly the same distance again.

Nothing! He must have felt a nasty prick in his jaw and decided not to grab again. There's another good pool a quarter of a mile downstream—the one which yielded my first grilse—we'll head there when you've fished this one completely. . . .

Here we are. Looks good, doesn't it? Main current again midstream through rock, but it stays streamy and attractive for thirty yards or more and most of the fish will be in the streamy water. Below, the pool widens out too much and becomes lifeless; and the tail end is all shallows and not worth a cast except in high water.

No wading here. You can walk quietly down the rocky bank as you cast. Don't think that just because the water is broken and lively a splashy cast 'banging' the flies down on the water will go unnoticed. Drop them gently, eight or ten yards away at first, gradually lengthening line as you move towards the wider, quieter water. Yes, that looks about right and you should be able to tell from the pull of the current on your line whether you are fishing at the right speed. Up with the rod tip a little. That's better.

Man, you're into one!

He should have hooked himself but the strain you immediately imposed would do the necessary if the fish didn't. Get back up the bank a little and lift more line out of the water. He's coming upstream nicely—but with a wriggling jump to set your heart pounding. It's a grilse : history repeating itself.

Now for some lateral pull to get him fighting again down the fast water. Keep the rod bent into him *all* the time. Ah, there's the dropper. I thought he was on the tail fly. It should be safe enough if you keep your point up towards the end of the fight when the fish is in the shallows.

Wheee! He didn't like your steady pull towards the shallows and fairly zoomed off across and upstream, and then back across river towards your bank. For goodness sake strip in that slack line and tighten on him.

He's still on. Maintain relentless pressure and don't let him dictate the fight for a moment, otherwise you may end up in the next pool like I did years ago! He's turning about quietly now. Walk him in towards me and I'll have the little gaff over his back in a moment.

Here he is! See how nicely that fly point has drawn into the corner of his jaw? Easy wasn't it? And you'll be able to take a bow in a moment. Three more anglers are on their way down to admire your shapely little five-pounder.

CHAPTER THIRTEEN

GRAYLING

THEORY

GRAYLING are fascinating fish. They belong to the salmon family, they have adipose fins, but look more like dace than trout. Their large dorsal fins with their colourful blend of mauve and red are beautiful. They are built for bottom grubbing, with small mouths typical of coarse fish; but they rise almost as readily as trout and often for much longer periods.

Grayling spawn in late spring—like coarse fish—and are at their best in the autumn, thus extending the fly fishing season considerably on those rivers fortunate enough to hold them. They are shoal fish, unlike trout, and when you have located several shoals you have found sport for a day. On most rivers outside the chalk country a pound fish is a good one and anything towards 2lb a whopper.

They are common in the north and certain rivers of Scotland, in the Peak district and Welsh border, and quite a few southern rivers, including Exe and Tamar. They were introduced artificially to many rivers, including those of the West Country, and on some chalk streams they are considered worse nuisances than salmon and slaughtered accordingly! I pursue trout during the early part of the season and turn to grayling around mid-August. From then until November, they are wonderful value and at times test one's skill and patience to the utmost.

Grayling thrive in rivers where there are plenty of pools and streamy glides: they avoid torrents and deeps which lack current. Like trout, they rise to surface fly and also take lures well sunk. Unlike trout, they rise virtually from the bottom of the river to take morsels from the top and such rises are disconcertingly quick.

One must respond equally quickly to hook them: this puts them in the dace category, while trout are slower and more chub-like.

Grayling tackle is trout tackle in almost every respect. I recommend a slightly finer cast to get the best out of their fighting qualities, and a few standard fancy fly patterns to restore morale when the grayling have waltzed around all your best imitations. Tinsel ribbing or a brightly coloured tag are advantages on a grayling fly. Useful fancies include Bradshaw's Fancy, the Witch, Red Tag and Bumbles of various colours; and I prefer not to be without my favourite little Blue Upright, a Red Quill and a selection of tiny Alders.

You can comb a big river with a lure and sunk line and attract some grayling. I've had them on salmon spinners and six-inch lobworms. This is not delicate enough to please me or most average grayling, however, and normally I use flies a size or two smaller than I should choose for trout in the same water.

Grayling will raise your hopes considerably by continuing to rise at intervals no matter how often the fly drifts over them. Sometimes you will rise one first cast (missing it, of course!) and fail to interest another for fifty more casts. If you rest them, and yourself, at intervals and continue casting quietly over them you will stand a good chance of picking up one or two.

Grayling don't like the sight of human beings any more than trout, but seem to take longer to panic. If you can see your fish, you will be able to judge the right moment to rest them. I'm sure grayling are frightened by drag on a fly, and they seem to be fussier than trout about the nylon cast—another good reason for fishing fine.

Most well-hooked grayling take the fly almost opposite the angler, probably from the side farthest from the cast. It pays to cast more across stream to grayling, when you would throw well upstream for rising trout. I've always found the fastest strike I could manage to be the best answer to the problem of hooking grayling, and that means a very much faster movement than the strike at the average trout. Sometimes the rise is an exciting splash or swirl: just as often it is a bubble or a quiet flick which makes the fly disappear.

When you hook a grayling you will be surprised how differently from a trout it fights. True, they do jump or thrash on the surface occasionally—particularly the big ones—and they do sometimes put their heads down and forge upstream; but on the whole they fight with an eel-like, backwards wriggling movement which makes you certain the light hook-hold is going to tear out if you bully them and pull too hard. Holding a big grayling in the fast tail of a pool is particularly awkward when it begins to tire. Your best plan it to get a little below it and work it inshore quickly, even if this does mean galloping down the bank.

Grayling early in their season are easier to hook and kill than September and October fish, and correspondingly less interesting. I consider them easier to catch in clear water although I have had them come to a fly during spates. Trout, by comparison, will take fly in quite turbid water conditions.

As the trout season goes out, and through October into November, much depends on the weather for pleasurable fly fishing for grayling. If it is warm and settled they continue to take surface fly freely. The first frosts may curtail their actual rising periods, causing them to start taking surface food later and cease sooner, but rise they will if only for a couple of hours at midday. Sunk fly and small lures should take them when they are not interested in anything on top.

Grayling can be taken 'blind', fishing the water in likely places with surface or sunk fly. It is, I think, better to locate rising fish if possible. Shoals tend to move about in the river more than, say, individual trout. Early in their season, from mid-June for some weeks, many grayling will be found along the shallow streams where they have spawned. Many a good fish will have been hooked out of season—though not intentionally, I hope, by true connoisseurs of the art of grayling fishing.

In small rivers the pools tend to confine them and the best places vary little. Medium and large rivers present their own problems of location; the height of the water naturally makes a difference to the position of the fish. Intelligent observation and a cautious and patient approach to your chosen stretch of river are the first essentials. Keep well down, either by crawling or wading deep, and throw your surface fly to the nearest risers, more across than up to show them as little nylon cast as possible.

The great secret in surface fly fishing for grayling is persistence—not fly pattern. Be prepared to continue casting over a shoal almost ad infinitum: a rise may come at any time. Eventually the grayling will tire of the game and begin rising some yards upstream or downstream of the area you are thrashing. This is a hint to discontinue operations and move to new water; you can return to the original shoal later and tackle them afresh.

Nymph fishing is every bit as effective as surface fly and should *always* be tried when the fish seem to be rising well but refuse surface fly. Their rises to nymphs are easily mistaken for honest sucks at surface morsels. The nymph is fished either upstream and across or down and across the river.

Grayling are partial to bright sunk lures such as Butchers and sometimes grab them with a solid tug. These lures—not too large, Nos 12 to 16 are about right—should be fished downstream either singly or two or three to a cast. When the weather is cold, and before and after signs of grayling movement on surface, this is a good method. Equally, it kills during the rise because the fly is *never* below the fish and out of vision. While I've often taken trout on surface flies whose hackles have the spread of a halfpenny, my preference for grayling are the smaller sizes, Nos 14 to 18.

It is worth remembering a first-class surface fly hackle can be nearly stiff enough to mask a small hook and prevent it lodging firmly in the mouth of a grayling, unless you strike firmly. Don't be afraid to hit the fish hard, its mouth is quite rubbery.

And now for a trip to the fringe of the Peak district, not so far from the River Dove where Izaak Walton's young friend, Charles Cotton, fished and wrote his famous addition to *The Compleat Angler* three centuries ago.

PRACTICE

It's 1 October, and what a glorious morning to lean against an old, stone bridge and breathe air as sparklingly clear as the water below. Just the morning to be planning an assault on the well-educated grayling shoals of two little Derbyshire waters.

We are going to try two brooks today, the Bentley and the

Henmore near Ashbourne. Both are Dove tributaries. The Bentley comes down from the Peak hills, a rush-and-tumble stream weired at intervals by stout logs. It has plenty of deep holes and a strong current. You shall try it until lunchtime, mainly with a sunk fly, and then drive a few miles across country to the quieter Henmore which flows through a flatter valley.

Both streams contain good fish. The Bentley has been more generous to me with trout: the Henmore with grayling. You must try and avoid trout today; avoid placing your fly in the obvious trouty spots; treat them with tender care if you hook them by mistake as you are bound to do occasionally.

On both these streams a 7ft fly rod is ideal. Tie a cast the same length, tapering to a last foot-length of 2lb b.s. nylon. The Bentley is overhung with trees and bushes. In places you will have to crawl and cast in cramped conditions. This afternoon on the Henmore you can enjoy casting without obstructions at your rear.

One small lure will be enough. If the Bentley was five times as wide it would be helpful to use a three-fly cast; but your fish will see the single lure here without doubt. A size 12 Butcher with its bright silver body and eye-catching red tag should do well. The line is a floater, and if you were fishing a nymph upstream I should advise you to grease the top four feet of the cast, too. You are going to fish downstream, though, and by feel rather than sight so there's no need for the grease tin.

There is a nice smooth glide fifty yards below the bridge and the last few yards are grayling water. Kneel on the shingle beach, well back from the edge, and cast across to the deeper water close to the far bank. The fly must sink immediately and come across the current 'bumping' their noses. If it doesn't go deep enough I'll replace it with one of my lead body patterns.

All's well, your fly is sinking sufficiently and you had a twitching take then which must have been a grayling. Didn't you feel anything or notice your line move slightly? You can't be leisurely with these fish: flick your rod tip up in a strike on suspicion only. No slack line, of course, that's handicapping yourself too much.

Ah! He took it just like a trout with a good thump on the rod tip. They *are* queer fighters aren't they? The beach you are kneeling on is ideal for drawing a fish ashore. Don't try and haul the grayling all the way back upstream; work it on to the gravel beach below you and crawl down to grab and kill it. With luck, you may get another fish or two from the same shoal.

Pretty little fish, just under $\frac{1}{2}$lb I suppose, which is about average. Grayling double that weight and more are killed here, but not often.

Into another? Well done. Don't allow it too much rope at the tail of the glide. It made quite a bulge in the water as it turned then, must be one of the better fish. Now it's trying to go down and pulling dangerously . . . and off!

Hard luck. You'll get used to it!

Let's have a look at another interesting pool where the stream turns left-handed and flows fast into an underwater jungle of tree stumps and brambles. Here you must wade deep to gain enough room to cast over the fast water below the turn.

That rise in midstream looked like a grayling moving. Ignore the deep area where the stream actually turns and put your fly across the steady, straight current three yards above the fish. Work down to him. You can give grayling a dozen casts in one place if you like, knowing there may be as many fish in the vicinity to take the fly. The water should be fished rather more thoroughly than you would fish it when trouting.

A tug, and up he comes in a flurry of surprise. That's one of next season's $\frac{3}{4}$lb trout. Pull him in *hard*; the less you play him the more strength he will have left when you've unhooked him.

No response from that midstream grayling, so let's go on down towards the farm bridge and try the long pool above it: it is long for this stream anyway, more than thirty yards. Don't bother about the first few yards immediately below the log weir, there are too many hungry trout there. Start where the sycamore grows on the far bank throwing its roots out in the water.

No . . . wait a moment. Two rises at once, and a third just afterwards. Here's a sign of movement worth watching a few minutes. It looks as if a nymph cast upstream would give better results. Slide quietly down the high bank into the water: it can be waded with care.

See? Two or three more movements; you can hardly call them rises because the fish aren't actually breaking surface. There's no doubt they are busily taking nymphs of some kind. Grease your cast to within 18in of its point and spit on this Pheasant Tail nymph for luck, and to sink it. Try the nearest grayling. Drop the nymph a yard above the rise and watch your cast closely.

You frightened that fish! It was a heavy cast, and as the water isn't more than three feet deep I'm afraid the 'plonk' disturbed him. The remainder of the shoal will be alarmed for a while at his sudden movement. Watch for the rises and start again when they become reasonably frequent.

That's better. Don't attempt to pull your line, let the current carry your nymph to the fish. The other way to fish a nymph is to cast downstream and bring it across the pools with little upward jerks like naturals swimming. If one method fails, try the other. You had a grand rise then but struck too slowly. Don't hurry to cast again, your line whipped back noisily on the strike and I expect the grayling are apprehensive.

I've seen several rises further up towards the little weir. You may pick up a fish if you are *very* careful, but they are bound to be wary. I'm told there are rivers where grayling congregate in mighty shoals and can be caught by the score. So can salmon in the Tweed! There aren't enough rivers of this calibre to go round.

Look at that! Just as you lifted the line to reel in a tiny grayling grabbed the Pheasant Tail almost at your feet. It's much too small to keep.

Well, you've had the best part of three hours on the Bentley, taken a brace and gained some idea of the difficulties of catching grayling from a hard-fished water. Now let's move to the Henmore. You can be starting there before one o'clock with several hours' fishing ahead. . . .

This brook runs through open countryside in a well-defined series of small pools connected by shallow runs. There is very little flow at low water and the grayling rise in the same places week after week in summer and autumn. Mind you, they're not the easiest of fish to catch: excellent training for a beginner.

It is mostly shallow water, even the pools are not much more than three feet deep. Every so often there is a lengthy glide, sometimes very shallow, where rising grayling can be spotted. These are the smaller fish shoals; the $\frac{3}{4}$lb specimens are often lone wolves, like trout, and you may pick them up instead of trout from the deep heads of the pools.

Surface fly here: this is just the day for it. We are bound to see some bubbling grayling rises in the pools.

Another farm bridge, and there's a very long pool above and below it. It must be over 100 yards long and, on a small brook like the Henmore, this means there is virtually no current for most of its length. The top twenty yards and a similar length at the tail end are all you need to fish unless grayling shoals are obviously elsewhere. You look upstream and I'll watch below the bridge.

A rise! You've seen one, too? Doesn't make much difference where you start, obviously. Tie on a size 16 Bradshaw and grease it well. In this very slow-moving current it will be sitting on the water for a long time between casts, and being a surface fly it *must* sit up well. Did you remember to knot an extra foot of 1½lb b.s. nylon on your nymph cast? Good, it's ideal for this placid pool.

You can start at the tail of the pool from the left bank, which is absolutely clear of obstructions. The right bank is higher, there are two hawthorn trees half way between the tail of the pool and the bridge, and the current—such as it is—flows nearer that side. You *cannot* walk boldly to the water's edge, or wade. If you intend catching grayling, you will have to crawl towards them and cast with infinite caution.

The rises begin about four yards from the tail end of this pool. About a dozen fish are active between that point and the lower hawthorn tree which just overhangs the water. Nothing is moving higher up towards the bridge. If you don't rush things, this short stretch of water will interest you for a good half-hour; and if you fish it *very* carefully you might come back to it at the end of the afternoon and catch another grayling or two. The important thing is to keep out of sight of the fish, and not to cast too frequently. *Always* credit fish with better sight than they possess, and a better sense of vibration: when I advise crawling I mean it, literally.

Grayling, like trout, seem to develop a rhythm in their rising; their rises come at fairly regular intervals. Throwing a fly on top of a rise isn't the best means of attracting a grayling. It is better to wait until you think the grayling is about to rise again before casting. Lengthen line until your fly drops a couple of feet above the nearest fish. Watch the fly intently. If your gaze wavers, sure as anything a grayling will nip up, take and spit it out before you have struck.

Try another few casts further across this time. Splash! Is he on? Bad luck, but it wasn't a sizeable one.

Pause a minute. Dry the fly and check the hook point. Crawl a yard or so upstream and send it over the heads of the two steady midstream risers. Their momentarily hooked sister hasn't alarmed them. That was a quiet, confident sort of rise and I'm not surprised you hooked the fish. The grayling has done its bit by wriggling away downstream and you can beach it without disturbance. Quite nice—just about ½lb.

More fly drying and sprucing of hackles: now try for that grayling's mate, still rising away happily. No good, but the fish is undisturbed. A change of fly might help. Put up this tiny Alder, size 17.

Good, that worked for once. Oh, and she's off. Never mind, you were the moral victor in that contest of wits. There are still two or three moving fish between your fly and the hawthorn tree . . . and for some reason they aren't impressed by the Alder. Try over them again with the Bradshaw's Fancy.

No, that wasn't a true rise to your fly. The grayling came up and bumped it, either because she turned away from it at the last moment or because she aimed at something else. Incidentally, grayling are just as likely as trout to pick natural fly off the water within an inch of your artificial, making you wonder whether they *did* rise to your fly. You could spend all afternoon trying these elusive fish, and end up getting one or two through sheer persistence; however, there's lots more water and some untried fish in it, so what about a move?

Let's go to the top of this pool. Once I hooked a grayling there which yanked my rod tip down and forged upstream like a 2lb trout, until the fly came away. Some stone blocks were put in to support the opposite bank years ago. The main current washes along them and your fly can be cast up and across as though you were trouting. The fly will bob down past the stones much faster than it moved at the tail of the pool. Strip slack line in quickly and be ready for instant action.

First cast: another nice grayling on the $\frac{1}{2}$lb mark. They have taken rather well for you in this pool. That fish fought just as hard as a trout.

Hello, you've hooked a trout. Shake out a yard or two of slack line and see if the fly comes free. And for once it has! Now reel up and we'll walk half a mile down the valley to another of my favourite pools. It's after three o'clock and soon we'll have had the best of the day.

Look at those rises! The grayling here are really enjoying life. They are rising where the fast current tips over an underwater ledge into the main pool; further down, where a large portion of the opposite bank has plunged into the river; and even on the shallows below that.

Move up opposite the crumbling section of bank. Drag is bound to be a tricky problem, so throw some slack line.

Two rises and both missed. They came very quickly indeed, I agree. What about a change of fly? There's still enough sunshine to bring out the glow in an Orange Bumble. . . .

Apparently it's not the Bumble's day. Try a final cast or two on the shallow run into the pool, and let the fly drift down as though washed along naturally by the current.

What a slash! Did you hook her? Oh dear, lost the fly in her jaw. That was certainly one of the better ones, maybe even a pounder. Your strike was too hard altogether at such close quarters and her weight and downwards plunge saved her.

The sun is dropping down into the mist now. The grayling won't be quite so keen to break surface. You might like to fish a 'dry' fly just awash, or change to a nymph. Towards dusk when the air feels chilly is the time for the deeply sunk lure. And while there's daylight, there's always hope.

CHAPTER FOURTEEN

COARSE FISH

SELECT them in whatever order you choose, only six coarse fish are consistent fly takers: chub, dace, perch, rudd, roach and bleak.

To any coarse angler accustomed only to catching these fish on bait, I strongly recommend light fly tackle as an alternative method on any hot summer day when all sensible fish are sunbathing instead of bottom feeding. Perch, of course, take sunk lures exactly like small spinners—thinking they are tiny fish—and will therefore accept lures at any time of year.

To any beginner who feels trout and salmon are the only quarry worth pursuing, I say try your skill on big chub in narrow, overgrown streams; try hooking two out of every three dace or bleak you rise; try bringing a pound perch safely to the net between weed beds.

Tremendous fun can be had from coarse fish, and they are especially valuable to fly anglers because, on the whole, they take a fly best when the salmon family are least interested in it—during the hottest summer days. Back to the water go all my coarse fish except sizeable perch, when the water can spare them, for perch are very tasty indeed.

Trout tackle will cope with any coarse fish, and let it be light tackle except for large chub.

CHUB

Seen in a clear river on a bright day, a shoal of chub might be mistaken for sea trout. Their dark backs and black tail fins, and the occasional flash of silver as one turns to take some morsel, all look infinitely trouty. The largest, which may weigh several pounds (the record, from Scotland, weighed over 10lb and five-pounders are caught every season) always lie at the head of the shoal and allow their younger brothers to be caught first and so give the alarm. Chub by the shoal, like sea trout, are not the easiest of fish to outwit.

Happily, chub do not spend all their time shoaled and basking in the sunlight. They cruise near the surface, in water varying from stagnant pools to fast glides and even rapids, and they can be very free risers indeed. Many chub are taken in error by trout and grayling anglers. Half-pound chub coming in rapid succession are no substitute for the fish with adipose fins! This is why chub have collected a rude name in certain quarters.

The dedicated stalking necessary to outwit chub of two, three and four pounds, falls into a higher category altogether. So does the plunging, hefty fight of such fish after a series of six-ounce trout. Chub do not fight as hard as fish of the salmon family, but their first throbbing run towards the nearest snag is not easily stopped and they will point their heads towards the friendly shelter of weeds or tree roots with real obstinacy. It is their first run that counts. If they don't succeed in beating you then you ought to win the fight.

Your 7ft trout rod is quite capable of subduing a grilse-size chub; but if you are lucky enough to have a good chub water at your disposal the 9ft rod would be a better choice, simply from its need to stand up to a lot of hard-pulling heavyweights. If you intend tackling big chub in confined areas of water your cast must be sea-trout strength, say around 5lb b.s. Select finer strains where there is room for the chub to move without danger.

Chub eat almost anything. They will take any fly from a smut to a mayfly and, being gourmands, they prefer large mouthfuls. Chub flies are designed on the principle of the-bigger-the-better. Big Palmers with fat, fuzzy bodies and brown or black hackles tied from head to bend on size 6 hooks are excellent at times. If the chub are shy of them, scale down to normal trout fly sizes; patterns aren't important.

Chub have large mouths, more like trout than grayling, and they rise slowly and take deliberately. Do *not* hurry your strike or your only satisfaction will be a huge flurry in the water as the fish takes fright. Once a fly hook has a hold in the fleshy jaws of a chub it doesn't easily come adrift, so play the fish hard away from its taking spot. Almost any method of fly fishing will succeed with chub. Surface fly and dapping give me most pleasure, but they will take nymphs and sunk flies or lures, too.

Chub thrive in many excellent trout rivers—to the discontent of some trout anglers—but they are also found in rivers like Severn, Thames, Trent and Wye, and I've caught them in a reservoir, too. They can even be caught on fly drifting down the broad reaches of rivers like the Severn in a rowing boat, and the lower Severn is *not* reckoned to be a fly river!

DACE

These are small but very lively, free-rising fish. Catch a half-pounder and you have a very good one; a $\frac{3}{4}$lb specimen is a whopper and one of 1lb a rarity. Small chub and large dace look very much alike, but the dace has a smaller head and mouth, looks more silvery, has less red colour about its lower fins and the anal fin (between vent and tail) curves inwards while that of a chub is convex.

Dace are invariably found in shoals and for the best results need the same cautious approach as chub. However, by concentrating on the nearer fish and pulling them downstream when hooked you can, on the right day, collect quite a number without frightening a shoal unduly. Tackle must be of the lightest to gain the best sport. They scrap well, better size for size than chub, but are too small to worry you or the finest of nylon casts.

Are they really worth catching? Of course, if only to sharpen your reactions for a spell of mountain stream trouting or grayling fishing. Dace rise extraordinarily quickly and have to be struck accordingly, although the largest of them will occasionally mouth a fly like chub with a slow, deliberate suck.

Small surface flies, or nymphs, are killing. Black is a good colour and sizes 14 to 17 are best. Dace aren't fussy about pattern, although they do at times concentrate hard on a particular hatch of natural.

Like chub, they are found in all sorts of rivers. Usk and Exe—

both splendid trout rivers—are infested with dace in their lower reaches; in the latter, they outnumber trout and grayling. They will rise in any river right through the summer and autumn, and into winter just as grayling do.

Normally, I fish a surface fly or nymph over dace shoals. Once on the rise they keep coming up, the rings of their rises spreading out in continuous, intermingling circles. Enough dace are caught on well sunk lures to convince me they have predatory instincts—like chub and large roach—and at dusk on a summer evening they will even rush at a large dragging sedge fished downstream.

Dace may seem light entertainment to serious trout fishermen, but I contend they are worth pursuing in their own right, and I've spent many a happy day trying to catch fifty and ending up contented with a dozen!

PERCH

Don't waste time trying surface fly for perch, which are predators and only interested in sunk lures. They are very beautiful fish, a dark green on top with black, tiger stripes of colour down their flanks. They have spiky dorsal fins, spikes on their gill flaps and large mouths which indicate their appetites. Perch are found in most British waters, flowing and still, but they are very little fished for with fly because spinners, lobworms and live bait are the acknowledged methods of taking them. This is no reason for not trying a fly at times.

Most of my fly-caught perch have come from an excellent trout reservoir where both species run big. The perch shoal in various deep holes and are reasonably easy to catch on Alexandra, Butcher or similar lures around size 10. I've never forgotten one greedy bounder of 1½lb which grabbed an undersized rainbow trout as I was drawing it ashore and held on with such determination that it, too, was dragged into the shallows and promptly netted!

Perch run to substantial weights, over 5lb very exceptionally, but I imagine the general run of fish on fly is ½lb to 1lb and you ought to be very happy with a two-pounder. As small fish they shoal in large numbers and I have often caught three small perch on a three-fly cast, the last occasion being on an Irish lough where

I hoped for a large trout. The trio took the first cast of the day as the boat drifted into the lough from its feeder stream, making me wonder for a moment whether I was into one good trout.

The flies must sink well to interest perch, preferably not far from weed, lilies or undercut banks; anywhere providing good cover and, in the case of rivers, no extremes of current. Sunk-line tackle is best, and where there is room for it you can cast a long line and give the flies every chance to hit on a shoal of perch in their travels. They can be fished back in exactly the way you fish for trout with lures, with slow steady jerks, but varying the pace if necessary.

Perch are active, twisting fighters. They are not as strong as trout but you may well mistake them for trout occasionally. Hooks don't always get a deep grip in their rather thin, gaping mouths so they should be played with a lighter touch than trout. And beware their spiky fins as you lift them from the landing net.

Perch don't show themselves much unless they happen to be chasing small fry. When you see tiny fish skipping out of the water in panic and some good swirls beneath, perch may be on the war-path. A large lure pulled fast across their noses may provoke a strike.

Undoubtedly you will meet anglers who will say lure fishing for perch is not *fly* fishing. Maybe it isn't, strictly speaking, but it's fun!

RUDD

These are very pretty little fish with golden flanks, red fins and small mouths designed for taking surface feed—their lower jaws protruding slightly by contrast with the roach whose upper jaws are more prominent, fitting them for bottom grubbing. I say 'little' fish, because most pond rudd in this country are fairly small and certainly average less than a pound.

They are essentially still water fish which roam about in shoals and move freely on the surface in warm weather. Where they grow large, 2lb and more, they are inclined to keep nearer the bottom seeking more substantial items of food than chance flies, nymphs, midges or larvae.

Floating line and surface fly or nymph is the drill, and the flies ought to be small, sizes 14 to 17. You will have no difficulty finding rudd shoals; invariably they advertise their presence just under the surface on summer and warm autumn days.

If a stationary fly fails to interest them, draw it slowly back towards you preparatory to casting again and it may produce a rise. Fly patterns don't matter a bit. A half-pound rudd fights as well as a dace, and it is easier to hook since it takes the fly in more leisurely fashion.

ROACH

Distribution widespread: weights, as far as surface-feeders are concerned, similar to rudd. The record is just under 4lb, and you aren't likely to tempt roach of much over a pound to fly, except on chalk streams in the mayfly season.

In appearance, roach are a cross between dace and chub, with a dash of rudd thrown in. They are not regular fly-takers, but a spell of settled hot weather does bring them up towards the surface of ponds and rivers where you may find shoals basking lazily in the heat. At such times a small fly, similar to your rudd and dace sizes, will persuade them to sidle up and bump it with their snouts. Sometimes you will see the fly positively pushed along the surface by an inquisitive but very cautious roach!

Use fine tackle and be in no hurry when fly fishing for roach. It is a slower game than any other form of fly fishing, and more river roach on fly are taken by accident than by design.

BLEAK

Finally, the smallest fly-taker of all. These silvery little fish infest some of our larger rivers such as Thames and Severn. They grow six or seven inches long and a ¼lb specimen would be a great prize.

For fly-fishing purposes they are warm weather fish. Shoals are easily spotted on the surface, their backs have a distinctly greenish tinge compared with the blue-black or brown of dace and roach.

Tiny flies, singly or in pairs or trios, are necessary. Bleak are not fussy about presentation and will take them drifting or dragging, afloat, awash or sunk. Treat them like dace, striking as fast as you can, and you may, on a prolific bleak water, count a day's result by the score. Catching them in this way may not rank high as sport, but it demands real dexterity and for light relief it is the ideal pastime on a hot afternoon when even the dace and small chub are moribund.

ACKNOWLEDGMENTS

The plates in this book were selected with the help of the Editor of *The Field*, Mr Wilson Stephens, and the Editor of the *Express & Echo*, Exeter, Mr M. C. B. Hoare, to both of whom I am very grateful. I also want to thank my colleagues on the *Echo*, Bert Davies and Dick Mitchell, for some of the photographs; Mr John Tarlton and Mr W. J. Howes for others which they have allowed me to reproduce; and Mr Ernest Petts of Newton Abbot who created the line illustrations.

INDEX

Page numbers in heavy type denote line illustrations or plates and are shown at the end of each reference.